Marketing Higher Education

Marketing Higher Education Theory and Practice

Felix Maringe and Paul Gibbs

 Open University Press

Open University Press
McGraw-Hill Education
McGraw-Hill House
Shoppenhangers Road
Maidenhead
Berkshire
England
SL6 2QL

email: enquiries@openup.co.uk
world wide web: www.openup.co.uk

and Two Penn Plaza, New York, NY 10121-2289, USA

First published 2009

A catalogue record of this book is available from the British Library

ISBN-13: 978-0-335-22032-8 (pb) 978-0-335-22033-5 (hb)
ISBN-10: 0-335-22032-0 (pb) 0-335-22033-9 (hb)

Typeset by Kerrypress, Luton, Bedfordshire
Printed and bound in the UK by Bell and Bain Ltd., Glasgow.

The *McGraw·Hill* Companies

To my wife Miniase and family and all those dedicated to the theory and practice of Higher Education Marketing

Felix

To those I love and the marketers who made the AM SIG happen

Paul

Contents

List of Figures and Tables

Preface

Higher education marketing is a growing field of practice, but may suffer from a lack of theoretical discourse. Early writers on educational marketing such as Gray (1991) and McMurty (1991) argued for the domestication or the development of a home-grown philosophy of marketing, rooted in the context of education rather than being some form of imported wisdom. Since then, we have witnessed a growing literature base on marketing especially in the developed world, yet very little seems to have been developed for education. In 1995, Foskett explored issues of marketing strategy within the secondary school sector and concluded that most marketing practice in UK schools was inchoate, underdeveloped and lacked a strategic focus. Towards the end of the 1990s, the education marketing debate shifted to issues of choice and student recruitment, following the expansion of education at various levels and the need to put 'bums on seats' in a more competitive education marketplace.

In that context, Helmsley-Brown (1999) undertook a study to investigate college choice in the further education sector and concluded that, although students initially base their choices on 'predispositions' and work within social and cultural frames of reference, young people also rely on the marketing information provided by colleges to justify their choices and to announce their decisions to others. This has led to a greater focus on marketing and communications strategies in institutions primarily aimed at attracting students to individual institutions. In 2003, Maringe, working on marketing in higher education institutions in the developing world, concluded that the marketing idea was ill-conceived even at the highest levels of university administration and that there was a disturbingly uncritical acceptance of the centrality of marketing as a key aspect of how universities functioned. In addition, he concluded that the growth of higher education marketing was seriously threatened by a range of factors which included a poor theoretical foundation for its development. In fact, a series of articles (Gibbs 2002; 2007) questioned whether marketing might not cause actual damage to higher education provision.

This book was conceptualized with these issues in mind and aims specifically to contribute to the theoretical discourse which is required to nurture the development of meaningful marketing practice. It is not a manual of marketing practice in the same way that many of its predecessors have been. Nor is it just another pretentious theoretical treatise of marketing. Most books align themselves with a theoretical position and deal logically with issues of practice informed through the lenses of the chosen theoretical discourse. This book is different: it has been written by two contrasting authors. One is a determined sceptic of marketing while the other is 'pro' marketing. Our belief is that by capturing these views in a single text we provide something for everyone. We are aware that such an approach is bound to involve controversy and possible contradiction, yet we believe firmly that no aspect of human endeavour is free of these attributes. It is enlightening to explore these in an as objective a manner as possible, especially considering it represents an approximation to life in today's higher education learning environment. We believe that many educationalists are cautious when they are presented with new ideas from other disciplines and agonize over whether to accept imported wisdom into their practice. This is the book for these people. It is both critical and accepting of marketing and brings together two models which we believe will work in the broadly sceptical field of higher education.

Several premises form the basis for this book, from which it presents key arguments. The first is that education is such an important element of societal development that failure to deliver its value to members of society denies society its right to self-determination and development. In short, we argue that because marketing is one way in which value can be exchanged and delivered, education needs to embrace the marketing philosophy as an integral part of its development and delivery.

Second, we argue that education should never be commoditized. It should not be seen as a piece of furniture in a shop with a price tag on it. It is both a process and product of interaction between the learner, the material of learning, the instructors or facilitators of learning, and the variety of resources used to aid the learning process. Yet, because it is so important, we think its value would more effectively be delivered with a marketing perspective. Third, we assume that marketing as a concept goes beyond the ordinarily accepted views of advertising and promotion. We argue in this book that marketing is about exchange and delivery of value between those who provide the educational service and those who seek to benefit from it. We thus see marketing not as a means to an end but as a process of building relationships based on trust and aimed at empowering the clients or customers of higher education.

The book is divided into two parts. Part I deals with the theoretical arguments surrounding higher educational marketing. Its aim is to open for discussion the notions of the market that are the source of marketing's inspiration. Such issues include marketing's contribution to the potential commodification of higher education, hence providing for mass participation through efficiency gains – but at what cost to a liberal ideal? Closely linked to the issue of market is the question of its participants' identities: scholars and students, or service providers and consumers? We discuss the potential incommensurate values of both the market and education. This leads us to try to develop a way to facilitate access to higher education that would avoid the wholesale encroachment of promotion participation by marketing. To illustrate this we coin the phrase 'pro-educating', a concept we deal with in detail in Chapter 3.

Part II is more practical, and consists of seven chapters dealing with a variety of what we consider to be the key issues which now face higher education institutions. We begin Part II with a chapter on institutional positioning and segmentation on the basis that, in order to deliver value to clients or customers, it is important to know in an intimate way the nature, composition and dispositions of the market served by the institution. The key argument in this chapter is that as the higher education marketplace becomes so keenly competitive, institutions will need to develop strategies that will help them to stand out from the crowd rather than operate in the shadows of competitor organizations. This is followed logically by a chapter on internationalization. In this age of globalization, it is imperative for institutions to develop an internationalization agenda. The chapter reviews both theoretical and practical issues of internationalization and explores some of the challenges which face institutions.

Chapters 8 and 9 consider the practical aspects of raising funds and pricing educational services. In current market conditions, being able to place a value on the education provided by an institution is a critical skill, both for revenue and for brand positioning. We discuss how we can price value in higher education and then consider why and how others might want to support these values and their outcomes.

Our research and that of others suggest that good institutional reputation is one of the major reasons students elect to study in specific universities. We devote Chapter 10 to issues of reputation and brand management. Many institutions only realize the importance of their reputation when it is in tatters. The chapter provides guidelines for managing institutional reputation and argues that managing a brand is as important as creating and developing it, and that this is a key aspect of delivering value to intended customers in the higher education market.

Our penultimate chapter deals with aspects of enrolment and enrolment management. We acknowledge the fact that this is perhaps the most important marketing function to which many people will tend to relate. However, in keeping with our belief that marketing is not just about recruitment, we have decided to place issues in this area at the end of the book. This is to emphasize the importance of enrolment, not just as a strategy of bringing students onto our campuses, but because it is an opportunity to deploy the strategies to deliver the greatest value to the students. The key argument in this chapter is that enrolment is not just about getting 'bums on seats': it is about creating value throughout the life cycle of the students' entire experience.

The final chapter is a reflective chapter which draws on our collective beliefs and arguments and attempts to reposition the idea of marketing and its role within higher education.

Note on the text

In this text we have used several terms that are defined in the Glossary. These terms are shown in bold on their first occurrence in the text.

Acknowledgements

In developing this work, we drew on our individual and collective research and understandings. We would like to thank first and foremost Alison Williamson who read the manuscript before it went to the publishers. Her attention to detail is second to none. We would certainly not have delivered this book on time without her generous advice, scrutiny and strict attention to detail. We are also grateful to our individual institutions at the University of Southampton and the Institute for Work Based Learning at Middlesex University for the support and encouragement given while this work was being undertaken.

There are also many people with whom we interacted in research projects who have informed our arguments in many different ways and to them we are extremely grateful. This includes in particular the membership of the Special Interest Group of the Academy of Marketing, set up and chaired by Paul, and now by Felix, for their support and inspiration. We would also like to thank Shona Mullen for her perseverance. Finally, we are grateful to our families, for being just that.

We hope you find this contribution meaningful and useful, and that it will be a basis for making decisions about marketing in your institution. We anticipate that our ideas will be challenged and shall feel that the work has been a success if readers begin to engage with it.

The Good Practice Checklist in Figure 9.2 appears with permission of OFFA.

Part I

Theoretical underpinnings

1 A broad overview of education marketing

Lenin might be an unexpected start to a book on marketing higher education, yet his works identify a major reason for the wholesale embrace of marketing by higher education. In a direct reference to Lenin's analysis of the privilege of the ruling class, and drawing upon it as a metaphor for university rectors, Lobkowicz (1983: 31) argues that universities have the tendency to be 'quickly overcome by the spirit of the age', that is, the spirit of consumerism. As today, during the eighteenth and nineteenth centuries they were imbued with a civic notion of utility. Universities began to open faculties and offer degrees in subjects such as engineering, chemistry and physics. These faculties and institutions certainly produced knowledge and innovation as well as new and radical perspectives on society, created and maintained in the service of the economy and functioning as the technological underpinning of industrial capitalism. It is here that we find the locus of the seemingly timeless 'crisis of the university', one that is still with us today. As Lobkowicz concludes, the persistent argument over the question of the purpose of universities stems from this basic philosophical contradiction. Should they produce wisdom or utility? Can and should they do both?

Universities not only express intellectual and scientific values directly through their mission of teaching and research, but also embody in their practice powerful organizational, instrumental values, and wider social and cultural values. As Bridges (2006) observes, these practices have already changed and still are changing radically and rapidly in most sites of higher education. For many years the university has struggled, hidden or diverted attention away from its role in a post-modern society. As the market has enframed and swept almost all before it, the university – or at least the traditional European university – has avoided clarity in its mission. It has managed, mainly through the luxury of state funding, to resist attempts to resolve the potential philosophical contradiction of whether it should produce wisdom or utility. Yet universities, it seems, are ever more reluctant to acknowledge these essential value structures. Scott et al. argue that 'scientific values are emphasized at the expense of more open-ended "intellectual" values; instrumental values, through which universities can demonstrate their utility, are fore-grounded at the expense of more critical.' Furthermore, 'universities now seem to wish to be regarded as technically contrived "service" organizations that willingly accept whatever values their key stakeholders (notably government and industry) seek to impose' (Scott et al. 2004).

The arguments are made stronger by the United Nations Educational Scientific and Cultural Organization (UNESCO) which, in its 2002 educational sector newsletter, spoke of 'Higher Education for Sale'. This theme, used by Symes (1998) and by Ball (2004), identified commodification fetish as a global issue which may well be unsuited to developed countries and even dangerous for developing countries. Further warnings are made by Naidoo (2007) when she concludes that commercial forces worldwide have propelled universities to function less as institutions, with social, cultural and indeed intellectual objectives, and more as producers of commodities that can be sold on the international marketplace.

The debate was recently legitimized in the UK by the 2003 White Paper *The Future of Higher Education* (DFES 2003) where much of the rhetoric has been on fees, their pricing and, since their announcement, bursaries. This debate has helped to gauge the elasticity of price and the degree of flexibility that institutions have in guiding their institution through the pricing mechanism. Pricing of goods for immediate consumption, for example cars, refrigerators and chocolate bars, is different from pricing services delivering an outcome created by the consumer and provider sometime in the uncertainty of the future. Purchasing such a service is an investment or a gamble and may be perceived in terms of behavioural transformation rather than price. This is closer to the discourse of the UK government when it argues the benefit of higher education in terms of internal, personal or social rate of return on higher education, but this is not the primary discourse in the market or, indeed of the government. The presentation of fees and bursaries has generally been represented by hedonistic images of consuming an education product in comfortable environments designed to evoke immediacy of benefit: it is a marketing approach which justifies the fees by converting education into utility, and then into something that money can buy.

In this *Zeitgeist*, the university has had to embrace the technologies of the market and consumerism; strategic planning with its emphasis on mission, vision and value, matching resources to opportunities and of course marketing. In a comprehensive review of the marketing of higher education in a globalized context, Helmsley-Brown and Oplatka (2007) identified an array of marketing tools and approaches applied to the market of higher education yet found that there is still research to be done to explore these models in context (2007: 364) which suggests at least a divergence from business applications. It is a world where the economy is not synchronized to a temporality that allows for learning, and the universities have turned their backs on a major part of what they used to be about: the inculcation of a capacity for critical thought through reflection and deliberation. There is just no time between the demands of the curriculum, assessment, enjoyment and economic work to do so. Student lives risk being untouched by their exchanges with the academy as they progress rapidly through their pro- grammes. Of course, such responses to consumerism will not be uniform across the field of higher education. As Naidoo and Jamasian observe:

> Universities that are in the upper levels of the hierarchy with high levels of academic, reputation and financial capital are likely to draw on superior resources to engage in practices intent on conserving the academic principles structuring the field of education, thereby maintaining their dominant position.
>
> (2005: 271)

In elite universities and departments around the world, students are least likely to push for changes because they understand that the combination of the university and the subject has a high exchange value in the external job market. By contrast, students studying loosely framed subjects in less prestigious universities are more likely to exert pressure on the faculty for change, and the faculty is more likely to be receptive. What this means is that the consequences of consumerism are likely to be felt more strongly at the more vulnerable institutions which admit students from disadvantaged backgrounds. In the long run, the fad will fade; the new programmes will siphon resources from the core mission, and the university's identity may grow murky. In contrast, the case of New York University (NYU) is an example of educational values predominating in the repositioning of the university. The campus was beautified, new facilities created, academic programmes and teaching strengthened, faculty appointments held to high standards and a solid marketing-and-communications effort was created to support it all. So, what of marketing?

Certainly, in this sense marketing has been recognized to be more than just advertising and selling. But do we know enough about learners' desires and aspirations to benefit from the utilitarian notion within marketing theory to explore and understand learners' requirements under the rubric of consumption? In a competitive environment, any increase in professional- ism ought to be beneficial but, if those efforts are misinformed by a metaphor of the market and developed under a 'philosophy of doing business' (Lafferty and Hult 2001), perhaps no progress can be made. All the above examples certainly share this theoretical underpinning, where a marketing precedent is followed and contextualized, without necessarily questioning its transferability or considering a better way to enable society to emancipate, to liberate and to allow higher education to flourish.

Education markets

Educational institutions are rapidly identifying themselves, both conceptually and in their discourse, as agents of national and international markets (Williams 1997). This is indicative of a general shift from a social policy that construed higher education as a 'public good' to one which is an extension of self-interested economic policy. However, while we acknowledge the influence of market forces, whether the structure of higher education should be a quasi-market, state-controlled or a directed response to competitive forces is not our concern. What we attempt in this work is to look at how marketing reflects these market forces and then to consider an alternative conceptualization which does not deny institutional rivalry, but sees it directed systematically by the players to secure primary benefit for the learner. This shift is associated with, but not fully explained by, a move from transactional, product-based market orientations to relationships based on long-term, symbiotic learning partnerships.

In traditional marketing texts and those on higher education marketing there is still an assumption that appropriate marketing can resolve the financial and competitive crisis that the sector faces, and appropriate marketing in this sense means identifying the audiences as consumers. This approach requires education to become a product delivered by service providers, a prerequisite which has not gone uncontested. Indeed, the extensive literature on models of students as consumers (summarized well by Eagle and Brennan 2007), indicates that such a standpoint is hastened by the adoption of fees. It encourages students to demand more for their money, either by virtue of an institution's reputation to secure the student an advantage in the job market or by the exchange value of their degree. Such models are, of course, countered and Clayson and Haley (2005), from the more developed fees market of the USA, and Lipsett (2005) and Waterhouse (2002) from the UK, argue for a partnership approach to learning where the student is one of several partners in the creation of education.

In this neo-liberal ideology of the market, we propose a different conception of the role of institutional engagement with the market. This is revealed in detail in Chapter 3. To emphasize education rather than the market we call it '**pro-educating**', a term derived from the desire to promote education for what it can contribute to society. We define pro-educating as:

> The mutually beneficial development of informed learning systems within which the development of relationships increases the opportunity for well-being and in which a duty of respect is owed and an obligation of fairness assumed.

In a recent article, Maringe (2005a) suggests that current university marketing lacks an appropriate contextualization, is poorly organized and co-ordinated, is largely responsive rather than strategic and that its application lacks formal operational guidelines. The CORD model, standing for Contextualization, Organization and co-ordination, Research and Development, provides a framework for raising the profile, the strategic focus and for developing a home-grown educational marketing philosophy.

Contextualization is a process that requires universities to understand in a more intimate way both the internal and external environments in which they intend to develop their curriculum. Organization and team building ensure that the marketing function becomes a grassroots process involving a diverse range of university staff. Researching the marketing interface allows developers to employ a variety of marketing techniques that enable the developers to devise a curriculum which not only reflects the needs and wants of potential customers, but can also make a valid claim for inclusion and incorporation in the new educational environment. The development phase encompasses a well-rehearsed cycle of curriculum development which includes trials and evaluation as integral aspects of the development process. As long as universities see themselves as either research centres or teaching academies, and fail to realize that ultimately these processes cannot be separated since they both contribute to curriculum development, the prospect of identifying with their core business will remain elusive.

There are no guarantees that this model will solve all the problems related to higher education marketing. However, it is certain that as long as we base our developments on imported wisdom, and as long as higher education does not identify its core business of curriculum development, it will be difficult to adopt the marketing orientation which it so badly needs. The CORD model thus represents an attempt to address the crisis that higher education marketing faces today.

The learner rather than customer approach encourages an overall goal for the marketing system to engage in collaborative resource allocation instead of divisive market-driven competition. Zineldin (1998) has developed a business model where business, let alone state-sponsored education, need not be viewed through the metaphor of war but can be viewed, in his words, 'as debate, co-operation and peace' (1998: 1139). In the social context, the market orientation debate has reduced trust in higher education, polarized the value of the reputation of institutions and damaged the collective perception of the level of the awards achieved by students. It has been dominated by a search for external accountability of standards, cast doubts on their validity and has fostered an unstable perception of the higher education sector where self-trust and validation once held sway, and in some institutions still do.

In response, the cornerstone of most marketing planning has been the 'four Ps' and the concept's expansion as an alliterative device. This has been a source of concern for some time, with Duncan arguing forcefully for us to challenge what he calls the 'tacit acceptance of the "Kotlerian thing", otherwise, it will insidiously continue to prevail and its prescriptions continue to be assiduously misapplied to education' (1989: 183). Bruner (1988) made an attempt at the time to confront the worth of this conceptualization of marketing in the context of education and replaced it with Concept, Cost, Channel and Communication variables. Still affirming the utilitarian notion of consumer maximization, there was a delay of more than a decade before Wasmer et al. (1997) felt that 'this approach better fits the situation found in higher education, in part due to its avoidance of the negative connotations associated with the for-profit, tangible, product orientation of the four P's'. There is, for instance, real debate on the use of the client/customer metaphor when it comes to assessment. For an interesting discussion of this point and other related issues, see Coates (1998). What is really needed is not the re-conceptualization of learners as anything other than what they are, but respect for what they want to be. This labelling is part of the institutions' own struggle for identity, manifested in their products and services. The shift in focus must be accompanied by a desire for greater understanding of the learner as part of their learning networks and communities. We identify three foci for such a re-conceptualization. These are: (1) learners' 'existential trust' in the learning process; and (2) learners' temporality, both of which could be applied to other interested parties in the higher education system. The third is learners' self-confidence as a learner and a practitioner.

The book's structure

Part I of this book deals with the broad theoretical issues regarding marketing; Part II focuses on more practical issues of implementation. The book differs from others on marketing for we perceive a problem using market-derived techniques used to promote education as we believe education has, or could have, different values to the market. Furthermore, we are not sure we can divorce the two. In what follows we discuss the issues of our notion of pro-educating and its development.

Having set out our position in this introductory chapter, we proceed in Chapter 2 to develop the argument further by addressing commodification and the service provider. In Chapter 3, we present an outline of our model of pro-educating, in Chapter 4, we take the students' perspective, and in Chapter 5, we discuss strategy issues in order to prepare the way for more practical work. This completes Part I.

Part II begins by considering the institution's position in the market-place, going on to deal with internationalization (Chapter 7), fundraising (Chapter 8), pricing (Chapter 9), reputation (Chapter 10) and enrolment (Chapter 11), before concluding with the role of marketing in Chapter 12.

We recognize that no book as slim as this can act as a manual to marketing, nor has it been our intention to burden readers with yet another. We have attempted, therefore, to raise issues that we feel are important to embrace in the development of higher education in ways that harness marketing, rather than allow marketing to enslave higher education. We hope this approach offers insight to practitioners as well as academe. Moreover, we hope our argument offers those who work in higher education a different way of looking at marketing and its application to higher education. We do this considering the marketing literature while maintaining an approach from the educationalist perspective. Our approach is not cynical of existing marketing; it is questioning. We are advocates of marketing providing it services the needs of higher education. This of course makes our task more difficult, as the role of higher education might not be obvious to all stakeholders. Certainly, public good seems to have lost its primary appeal, to be replaced by individual personal benefit. We do not claim this is solely due to marketing, but perceive that its techniques have a case to answer. In this book we hope to investigate this in order that marketing's benefits to the promotion of the education that institutions have to offer can be maximized.

2 The commodification of marketing

In the past 20 years or so, higher education has undergone a major transformation in support of the knowledge economy. Throughout Europe, the general trend has been towards the erosion of the social contract. The underlying direction of change has been towards efficiency, driven by competitive forces both within existing and between new providers of higher education. Technological changes have fuelled the globalization of higher education with the General Agreement on Trade in Services (GATS) likely to accelerate the trend of transforming higher education into a commodity that can attract international customers and, through private investment, compete on a global scale.

We begin by defining what is meant by **commodification** and non-commodification. Here, commodification refers to the production and delivery of goods and services for monetized exchange by capitalist firms in pursuit of profit. In Marxist political economy, commodification takes place when economic value is assigned to something that traditionally would not be considered in economic terms, for example an idea, identity or gender. Such 'commodity fetishism' (Ball 2004) goes beyond the notion of consumption which typifies our everyday lives and again, as Ball states, we are 'denying the primacy of human relationships in the production of value, in effect erasing the social' (2004: 2).

As such, commodification has three constituent components, all of which must be present for it to be defined as commodified: goods and services are produced for exchange, exchanges are monetized and monetary transactions take place for the purpose of profit. For exponents of the commodification discourse, therefore, contemporary economies are characterized by one mode of exchange replacing all others. In this view of an increasingly hegemonic capitalism, the commodity economy becomes the economic institution rather than one form among others of producing and delivering goods and services. Does this sound like higher education to you? To commentators such as Wilmott (1995, 2003), it certainly raises issues about the essential values of higher education in the development of the student as a person and as a carrier of culturally valued knowledge. It seems to him that this development is being replaced by activities devised to increase the exchange value in terms of resources that will flow to form external metrics such as research assessment exercises.

Knowledge economies

The notion of a knowledge economy is widespread and as such we shall limit comments here to key points relevant to the argument regarding higher education. The notion of a knowledge economy has emerged to account for the transformation in the Organization for Economic Co-operation and Development (OECD) countries from industrial to post-industrial economies. Rather than focusing on the production and transformation of raw materials, as was the case in the past, new information and communication technologies and increasing **globalization** allow 'knowledge economies' to focus upon knowledge-intensive activities: the production, processing and transfer of knowledge and information (Nowotny et al. 2001). The currency of knowledge economies is novelty, or innovation; the emergence of new ideas and new ways of doing things. As a consequence, knowledge, once considered a scarce resource, has proliferated into 'information' and into a marketable product. In a knowledge economy, knowledge is valued for its potential to generate economic development and prosperity through innovation. This instrumentalization of knowledge has meant that the kind of knowledge that is particularly prized in a knowledge economy is that which is readily transformable into marketable products and services. This re-situating of knowledge as a tradable product radically changes the role of university research. As Nowotny and colleagues have argued, a new set of demands is being made of universities, so that knowledge is increasingly being produced for, and in the context of, application.

The notion of '**mode 2 knowledge**', a term coined by Gibbons et al. (1994), points to a blurring in the past of the division between knowledge 'creators' and knowledge 'consumers', where the academy was equated with the former and industry and the professions with the latter. As Nowotny and colleagues point out, this has created a context where a university's research is increasingly contextualized and packaged for trade.

The demands of 'application', or the usability of knowledge, are increasingly influential in determining what is researched and how, particularly through the research funding arms of government. Policy initiatives on the part of governments are increasingly aimed at promoting education and research in the 'key innovation areas' of information and communications technologies, mathematics and science. This creates tensions in university environments where knowledge has traditionally been pursued for its own sake (Readings 1997).

The OECD sees universities as playing a key role in strategies for building a national innovation system. The logic of economic growth through the creation and transfer of knowledge is both persuasive and pervasive. But are other benefits of a renewed emphasis on 'applied knowledge' being overlooked? What other reasons might there be for reasserting the value of knowledge that emerges through and is relevant to practices that are not reducible to economic value? We consider this a form of de-commoditization where we turn the instrument of the market – marketing – onto itself to work against the dominance of the marketing and realize the liberating notion of education we spoke of in the Introduction.

The term 'commodity', as used in management literature, does not assume the tightly defined notion of the economist but is used more freely to mean a packaged, consumable product capable of being considered a component of the market mechanism. It has become part of the corporate discourse of the academy as it finds its place in the knowledge industry, where the university is a revenue generator, where its intellectual capital is a resource, an asset to be leveraged, and knowledge itself becomes a commodity to be produced and traded in a market where academic endeavour and students are the content. But this use is ever more dangerous in an educational context, for it seduces the educationalists into devising marketing-orientated offerings in place of education. In doing so, it confirms the transformation of education into business and, with it, the origins of its creation.

Seeking to turn education into a commodity, framing it in market terms and encouraging the entry of commercial concerns could be seen as simply an expression of neo-liberal politics in a particular country. However, we need to understand the nature of the forces that have pushed governments into adopting such policies – and it is here that we can see the process of globalization directly at work. This might be conceptualized as a fundamental attack on the notion of public goods, and upon more liberal ideas of education. Learning has increasingly been seen as a commodity or as an investment rather than as a way of exploring what might help lives flourish.

Doti (2004) has described colleges and universities in the USA using price as a discriminator of their product, claiming that price is the discriminator that distinguishes the higher education market from a commodity market. He argues that this ability is being lost and, if this is the case, that higher education is becoming more like a commodity. His empirical study suggests the practice of balancing fees and rebates to attract students is declining, although at different rates. Thus the more selective universities retain a greater edge of discrimination values in financial terms than the majority, which cannot aspire to such a policy and decrease fees and increase discounts when they see their returns decline over time. This represents a financial argument to resist the market forces of commoditization – there are others.

Furthermore, the operating principle of the market tends to hand over the moral responsibility to the market-making educational services for more attributes than are appropriate. Should the following attributes be mediated through a market mechanism: tolerance; justice; and protection of the vulnerable? Moreover, the reaction speed of the market should surely have a different pace to that of a commodity market; time to contemplate, reason and deliberate rather than simply assemble information, draw the most obvious self-interested conclusion, then act.

In this sense, we envision the commodification of higher education somewhat as Standish (1997), reflecting on the use by Heidegger of the concept of '**ready-at-hand**' and '**present-at-hand**', comments that when functioning correctly, things become what they are when used, not when they are observed. It is only when they malfunction that their contribution is really perceived. This awareness allows us the possibility of re-relating to things and seeing their wider potential. The point is that if education becomes no more than a taken-for-granted, instrumental service which is ready-at-hand, personal engagement is limited to its perceived use. The educative process can reveal the potential of what is ready-at-hand through allowing us to become involved in ways which are more than treating that which we encounter as mere equipment for something. There is a danger that students may 'come to think of themselves in terms of sets of compe-tencies aptly summed up in standardized records of achievement, and to see education in these limited terms'. Further, the 'supposed priority of the student's autonomy is emphasized through the principles of the negotiated curriculum and the students' ownership of learning ... where the student selects from a variety of prepared packages and where learning is, in fact, resource-driven' (Standish 1997: 453–4).

This reduction of the students' learning experience from a holistic one, where they form their future from the decisions they are able to make, to one of training students to fit into one predominant role, is paramount in the shift from Sartrian learning-for-itself to learning-for-others. It is the produc-tion model of education best suited to central control and planning. Accompanying this shift is the real risk of students facing the angst of their existence alienated from their authentic beings.

If this reflection is to be genuine, however, it requires a sense of self-assuredness to the authentic facing up to the anxieties resulting from fear of personal finitude. This facing up can threaten to reject the social world and it is the management of this process, without inappropriate loss of both self-concern and being-with-others that is, we propose, an element of education which can claim common assent from those involved in it. This communal involvement in the self-authenticating of members of the community helps oneself to find meaning in the everydayness of its existence: students would feel sufficiently at home to be prepared to risk reflection on themselves as becoming, rather than being. As Bonnett proposes, 'A concern for authenticity would lead to a shift of emphasis in which education is regarded as a process in which the expression and development of the individual through the acquisition of authentic understanding is central' (2003: 60).

Many universities are now responding to the demands of professional people at work. In the past ten years there has been a steady growth of professional doctorates (Scott et al. 2004) and master's degrees that focus on professional areas of learning. Universities have embraced the ways of managerialism in many respects and under the influence of technology (see Heidegger 1977; 2000) have distanced themselves from a *paidea* of education, of knowledge and conduct towards the instrumentality of securing work. This has been argued in many places (e.g. Readings 1997; Aronowitz 2000; Bok 2003) and could, as predicted, lead to the self-destruction of the university as it competes in a knowledge economy with commercial research institutions and proprietary training organizations (e.g. Microsoft). In this respect it could be argued that work-based professional studies ought to offer a route to the revitalization of the university's research considerations. This is needed because of a decline in the focus of universities due to the fragmentation of their endeavour, based upon the specialized ground-plans of the disciplines and the objectification of beings into the entities of research.

A further difference is in the form of knowledge that the context of application creates. It has been acknowledged as being very different to knowledge that is researched in the more conventional way and has been described by Gibbons et al. (1994) and others (Nowonty et al. 2001) as 'mode 2' research. Within this mode of research, there is also a considerable and growing body of literature that addresses research undertaken by practitioner researchers. Robson (1993) discusses the advantages and disadvantages of being a practitioner researcher, and Gray (1991) briefly examines their possibilities and limitations. Gray then relates in more detail how practitioner researchers who are insiders and use the methodological approach of action research can easily become implicated with ethical issues.

Globalization and commoditization

Shaw (2005) claims that trade in higher education has been intensified by the rapid growth of newly established universities and colleges in the Middle East and North African region and in South-East Asia, both state-financed and private. Many of these are strongly oriented to the provision of specific courses, notably in vocationally related areas such as English language, management, paramedical services, media and information technology. Trading in knowledge, then, is big business: organized, thoroughly commercial and part of the global capitalist market. It well deserves detailed local research. Higher education is a valued international commodity and the idea that higher education is a commercial product, to be bought and sold like bananas or airplanes, has reached the global marketplace. The World Trade Organization will be considering a series of proposals to make the importing and exporting of higher education subject to the complex World Trade Organization (WTO) protocols and that would free international education from most current restrictions, many of which are designed to ensure its quality and to maintain national control over higher education. As a practical matter, WTO accreditation excludes some providers from offering higher education services, and it involves a somewhat arbitrary application of a constantly evolving set of regional standards.

It is against this background of changes and developments that one must consider the GATS and its implications for the world of higher education. Adopted in 1995 under the WTO, GATS clearly identifies education as a service to be liberalized and regulated by trade rules. While its supporters see GATS as an opportunity, others view it more as a threat. For some, the notion of higher education as a tradable commodity is a challenge to the traditional values of higher education – especially the idea of higher education as a public good and a public responsibility.

More universities and new for-profit companies will export academic and professional programmes as a commodity to a variety of student populations. There are already some noticeable differences among national policies in this domain. Australia, the UK and Canada are more oriented to the international market (Ryan 2002). Many of their universities try to export their higher education as a commodity to Third World countries. American universities are more directed inwards, generally preferring campus-based integration of digital technologies, with a few examples of purchases and partnerships in physical campuses overseas.

The inclusion of education in free trade agreements has given rise to a major controversy in the world of education, as is apparent from the numerous campaigns – and other institutional responses – that have been organized in recent years to demand that education be left out of the free trade agreements. At the same time, a large number of empirical studies and theoretical analyses have been carried out on the problems associated with the commercialization of education services. These studies have addressed a wide range of issues, such as the inclusion of trade agreements in the concept of 'global governance of education' (Robertson et al. 2002); the fact that trade agreements have acquired formal sovereignty over certain aspects of national education policies (Robertson and Dale 2002); and the reasons why such agreements deepen the existing inequalities between northern and southern countries (Altbach 2004).

Sir John Daniels' view (2005) is supportive of the globalization commodity argument. He argues that when products become commodities, there is fierce price competition between manufacturers and profit margins are squeezed. Producers dislike this and industries often have to restructure, but consumers benefit greatly.

Specifically, when querying the implications for education and asking whether the commoditization of learning materials is the way to bring education to all, Sir John's answer is:

> Yes, it is, and 'open' universities in a number of countries have shown the way. By developing courseware for large numbers of students they can justify the investment required to produce high quality learning materials at low unit cost. Such materials can be used successfully outside their country of origin after local adaptation and translation. Commoditizing education need not mean commercializing education. The educational community should adopt the model of the open source software movement. We can imagine a future in which teachers and institutions make their courseware and learning materials freely available on the web. Anyone else can translate and adapt them for local use provided they make their new version freely available too.
>
> (Daniels 2005)

Sir John's views (2005) are supported by Czinkota (2004), who claims that there are a number of reasons why higher education should be liberalized in the GATS:

- Knowledge is crucial to advancement anywhere around the world.
- In spite of much support and goodwill, higher education remains a privilege or is entirely elusive for a large proportion of the global population.
- The key constraint to progress is not the availability of knowledge but its distribution, absorption and application. In its role as a global channel of distribution, higher education has become a bottleneck.
- Major funding and productivity enhancements are required.
- International competition offers the key opportunity to boost productivity and attract resources.
- Institution and programme mobility will be particularly instrumental in global capacity building.

Pierre Sauvé of UNESCO, on the other hand, recognizes that there is a danger of 'McDonaldization' of higher education with the spread of a single formula on the Western model. He suggests that, when

> faced with increased competition, universities are tempted to invest in subjects that are going to be most profitable for them, to the detriment of less profitable ones such as human sciences. They will also be tempted to move more and more towards doing research that pleases their funding sources. In the future, parents will have to spend a greater part of their income on their children's education and that will only increase social inequality.
>
> (UNESCO 2002)

We argue that, while convenient, the notion of commodity is unhelpful and misleading when applied to education. Unlike other commodities, education already has the attributes that satisfy consumers' needs to a great extent in any sense. The job of the marketer is not to simplify the selection but to widen consumers' notions of what is available. This is not a process of a limited provision of the same product in a series of differently coloured boxes, but of realizing demand for education, not accreditations. Shifts in consumers' needs as they manage their relationship with the modes of production will demand that marketers use the power of the brand as a lever. Failing to do so will force marketers to seek lowest-cost provider status, to compete against other goods or services primarily on price, and to realize no more than commodity margins. As Doyle (1998: 35) comments, technology has 'had the effect of first "commoditizing" then making obsolescent the products of companies that are not staying ahead'.

Resisting commoditization for the sake of education

The idea behind the concepts of commodification and de-commodification is that the development of modern capitalism transferred 'labour' into a commodity so that income and survival depended on labour market participation. The establishment of such a context which can both match and confront expectation is, however, a dangerous business. Particularly for those new to the discourse of higher education within higher education institutions, the danger lies in society's value-laden practices which have invaded the truth-seeking ethos of Jasper's ideal university. Higher education institutions owe a responsibility of critical self-scrutiny both to themselves and to their present and future communities whose adults are, or will be, entrusted to them. In this project they will need to accept that its students are vulnerable to the reality defined for them. That reality imposes an obligation upon higher education institutions to reflect on the values of their host communities and, through their own autonomy, offer students the choices associated with the development of authentic, autonomous decision-makers. As Wilcox and Ebbs state: 'The relationship between students' attitudes and values and the environment that supports or challenges them stands as a dynamic dialectic of confirmation or rejection that affects the ethical positions and choices of both the individual and the institution' (1992).

Nentwich (2001) raises some very interesting issues regarding the commoditization of academic knowledge through the issue of copyright and academic journals. Basically, the argument is whether specialized academic information should be understood as a commodity intended to generate revenues, or whether access to scholarly information is a social good that must be freely available. Contextualized in the educational arena, the argument is at the core of what commoditization is and why there can be a case for de-commoditization. Essentially it concerns the loss of the social good in the valuing of production. Returning to the Nentwich example, the case for de-commoditization of the academic work involved removing those whose primary interest is in the revenue value of knowledge. If the work that is being conducted is the production of academic articles for dissemination, what actually does the publisher do to transmute the academic work into one that has an exchange value never intended in its product? Nentwich believes it is not a great deal and argues for open and free distribution through the universities themselves of the knowledge created by their academics as one way of de-commoditizing the process.

Useful as this strategy may be, it will fail if the institutions are themselves intent on commodifying for their own benefit. The answer seems to be to view the problem from a perspective other than the market, from where value is more intrinsic and education offers both an economic and social good made manifest in the freedom of ideas.

Prior to 1992, undergraduate and post-graduate degrees were built into strong brands by a small group of universities whose influence was beneficially reflected in the other members of the university sector. This halo effect has now been diluted to such a point that its original value is being questioned. Global positioning is not possible for all or even for a large minority of UK universities. Once the link of the ubiquitous honours degree has been re-positioned as a thing of value only from certain universities, many new and mass institutions are rapidly left without a concept to offer their publics. Indeed, this change would happen more rapidly if universities were able to charge their own levels of fees.

The marketing of higher education ought to be about de-commoditizing its offerings, not commoditizing. It should seek to integrate product and service, and combine both in an inclusive package to encourage future growth by de-commoditizing current offerings. A precedent is seen in banking, a service traditionally based on complex structures which have been commoditized to make them plainer to the consumer. The result is a commitment to serving customers' needs by providing superior service and niche products. Yet many banks are decoupling the complexities of their products to reveal the costs. They earn profit by making what they actually do seem clear, but not simple, to the customer. Similarly, higher educational services could become an internationally tradable commodity within an increasingly competitive global market. The process of de-commodification of higher education should borrow from the marketing knowledge without being seduced by its non-critical discourse. Whether or not communication should be totally transparent needs careful development and theorization.

Marketing synthesizes a notion of value beyond that of an experiential world and this makes us overseers rather than participants in knowledge creation. A consequence is to displace experiential meaning, as technology leads us to discard value and behaviour becomes a means to an end, losing its potential to hold intrinsic meaning. This clearly has ramifications for the world of being: as we abstract ourselves from our world, our notion of being becomes world-less. We behave as we think scholars should, and induct students into a learning community where neither they nor we know what scholarship is.

Young (2002) offers the example of the bureaucratic, machine-like modern university in which it is no longer customary to find teachers and students but rather 'suppliers' and 'consumers', with all that this system entails. He adds that in modernity, to be is to be an item of resource. Fitzsimons (2002) and Standish (1997) have articulated similar views of the impact of enframing on education. Yet it is in Clegg (2003) that the full expression of the changes in temporality in academic setting is expressed, and this is discussed in Chapter 3.

The purpose of the application of forms of knowledge is, we think, very different for marketing and education. Marketing aims to achieve predetermined ends and it does this by applying marketing skills and technologies. It has a tangible goal: market share, sale volumes or profit. This is quite unlike the development of an educated person and here we distinguish 'educated person' from an academically-accredited person. The accreditation goal is indeed more similar to a marketing goal and this notion of education is rapidly replacing the idea of an educated populace with that of an accredited one. Indeed, we believe it is in this sense that the government interprets participation levels in the UK, perceiving it as a marketing problem rather than one for education.

We are less critical of marketing skills *per se* than the unguarded consequences of their application. If we allow a consumer marketing concept to create a form of educational experience appropriate to marketing techniques, then we allow authentic well-being, revealed through education, to be compromised by the totalization of the marketing concept. We become something, rather than someone, and consumption of the known holds sway. This is inappropriate under a self-transcendent notion of education.

This debate has been rehearsed, to some extent, in the social marketing literature. There, Peattie and Peattie have developed the argument that we need 'a more thoughtful and selective application' (2003: 387) of marketing principles. They are not alone in this stance. See, for example, Gibbs (2002), Janic and Zabber (2002), Wasmer et al. (1997) and Brownlie and Saren (1992). The last two authors state that there has always been a paradox: 'marketing techniques are used by firms as much to influence and manipulate consumer demand as to identify and anticipate it' (1992: 41). They have all supported the view that the ideology of marketing, constructed in the commercial era of the 1980s, is problematic when applied to other areas of human endeavour where the market might not always hold sway. In short, marketing of higher education should not be about manipulating recruitment and demand. Rather, it should reflect a deep-seated desire to deliver value to those who seek to engage with it. ***Techne*** (the emphasis on outward manifestations and technical competence) should be subservient to ***poiesis*** (the fundamental desire to change the human condition for the better.

Education as being, not consumption

Marketing's influence on the way we view ourselves has been well charted, e.g. Featherstone (1991), Richins (1994) and Brown (2001). Less well explored are the consequences of marketing in the odyssey made by community of scholars towards its members' well-being as healthy, authentic and worthy individuals. We make sense of our lives authentically by revealing ourselves meaningfully in our actions, for example, consumption. All too often it becomes the principal mode of revelation – consuming a book, getting the course out of the way or passing the last module in the series. Marketing transactions can be exchanges of meaning, but are more often presented as exchanges of value stripped of any but the value they bring to the parties. Thompson, in his significant contribution to the subject (1997: 438), argues that 'interpreted (or perceived) meanings are fundamental to marketing's core interests', but this is only correct if marketers respect meaning and have the means and dispositions to understand these meanings and act upon them. Thompson offers such a way when he suggests hermeneutic frameworks to interpret the meanings of consumption in relation both to a consumer's sense of personal history and a broader narrative context of historically-established cultural meaning. This is the educational transformation we refer to when we talk of payment rather than an exchange of value.

The technological world of planning seeks to populate the future, to make it a linear extension from the past through to the present, usually by extrapolation. It 'owns time' through the hegemony of determinism and it thus ignores the heuristics of the decision-making of a multi-faceted potential student population. How else could we seek to anticipate rather than guess what will satisfy consumers' requirements? This rationality seeks to transcend the reality of these heuristics and stands as a signifier of reliability, competence and prudence. Such implicit application moves marketing away from a creative endeavour into the nihilism of determinism, of a time devoid of temporality and where the *techne* of planning is used without the need for the wisdom of experience as it relates the revelation of what is being marketed. This is the new marketing myopia.

However, as indicated later, with regard to the issue of fees, it is up to institutions how they pay the bursaries to students. According to OFFA:

> The majority have said they will be paid to students in cash, but some will be in kind, either in addition to cash bursaries or as standalone offerings. For example, some students could expect to receive travel passes, laptops, vouchers for bikes, sports centre passes and art equipment.
>
> (OFFA 2005)

This is a neat marketing ploy, but hardly worthy of a long-term, developmental notion of education. The student may be dissatisfied if the rigours of education do not match the expectation created in the marketing hype used to cover the fees issue.

Summary

The challenge that we face is to de-commoditize higher education. We believe that a marketing concept that respects the benefits of social and economic capital offers such an opportunity. In marketing theory, the commodity is an indistinct product for which there are many suppliers and many buyers, which is traded in a market where the price is variable and supply and demand are elastic. In this simplification, the market behaves in a way that will balance supply and demand, however, it is accepted that this is not typical behaviour. Markets are distorted by supplier intervention to build and support brands which are differentiated in consumers' minds and which attract prime prices over generic products by offering perceived value. The idea of selling the commodity of higher education is thus a little over-worked, as brands already exist. We are not against brands but feel that distinct forms of higher education have become homogenized in a collusion of mediocrity based on immediacy, hedonism and financial return. The position of higher education is such that it does not encourage institutions to resist the scrutiny of the market, to confront the model and overcome commodification. In the pages that follow we hope to show how the right tools in the hands of the educationalist can achieve the desired de-commodification.

First, we discuss the roles of the main actors engaged in the creation of education and what they might do to resist commodification. What can they do and how should we conceptualize their contribution to education? Quite simply, we ask whether students are defined as customers and academics as service providers. Do these labels sit comfortably with the values and ethos of higher education?

3   Marketing as pro-education

In the last twenty years, however, [the university] has metamor-
phosed rapidly into a completely different institution – if such a
perpetually mobile business-oriented entity may still be called an
'institution'. So radically has the university changed that the typical
academic, administrator or student from the 1960s and 1970s would
barely recognize it today. It might seem to them to be more akin to
a marketing company or advertising agency, so concerned is it with
profit, products, clients, market share, branding and image.

(Hassan 2003: 79)

Premise

For Aristotle, there appears to have been a distinction between a specific
form of making or production, *poiesis,* and the more general notion of doing
and being involved in an activity that is ***praxis***. This, in the case of
education as ***paideia***, for example, would relate to ethics and politics.
Aristotle's argument is that something's function is for its end.

Praxis is encapsulated actions which promote wisdom, practical wisdom based on the notion of acting in ways which are for the good and the
well-being of self and others: at least that is the reason that Aristotle gave for
seeking through enlightenment – educating towards happiness – the highest
good of happiness. However, this distinction between *praxis* and *poiesis* as
different ways of being-in-the-world has become blurred, as *praxis* has been
essentially '**enframed**' by the technologies that dominate and surround us.
They threaten to turn *praxis*, with its potential of wise well-being, into the
utility of *poiesis*, collapsing means into ends. (See Heidegger for an extended
discussion of the relationship between these concepts.) Marketing should not
be about concealing or merely altering people's perceptions about education.
Rather, it is about developing fundamental change in people's ideas about
the world, bringing and delivering real value to their lives.

If we apply the above to being-in-the-world of education, both in
concept and in practice marketing functions as *poiesis* and, as it is in the

market, it produces commercial value – as in Heidegger's discussion of being in-the-world in *Basic Writings, Problems of Phenomenology*. The purpose of marketing in its essence is derived from its practical relationship with its end – the market – and, through that, neo-liberal notions of capitalism, manifest in the creation of commercial value in and of itself. The marketer is enframed by the essence of marketing technologies to this end. And so when these techniques and practices, which are derived from the market, are applied to education, they enframe education as a utility. The argument is that marketing techniques, for the most part, cannot be divorced from the genesis of the utility of the market, regardless of the sentiment or wisdom of those using them.

One of the consequences of education so marketed is the promotion of higher education as a means to an end and not an end in itself. Thus:

> The technological project's focus is on securing an end, its attitude towards temporality is that time, in its unruliness, must be domesticated, and must be brought under control. Opposed to this, praxis fully recognizes time as its field of action and as an enabling medium – for instance, the meaningful action of praxis as an application or repetition of the past understood as an historical legacy – and seeks, ideally, to maintain the singleness of individual identity through the vicissitudes of temporal existence.
>
> (Simpson 1995: 57)

The argument thus prevents higher education, if marketed, from being promoted as a place for education where education is considered as anything other than an end of the market (Gibbs 2007). Many would argue that this is its role; to reflect the values of the society in which it serves. We would not dispute that this is a position worth holding in a diverse higher education field of endeavour, but we would argue that the mass use of this approach ought to be resisted, for it reduces choice, potentially inhibits critical thinking and ultimately leads to a loss of democracy. However, given the power of the market, the voice of dissenting institutions still needs to be heard and the resistance needs to be visible. To do this requires such institutions either to formulate marketing for education in ways which do not lead to the deconstruction of education to a marketable value, or to find ways of promoting education which are found outside the domain of existing marketing theory.

Temporality

Common to most approaches to this problem is the notion of an abstract, absolute, linear, irreversible, monotonic, homogeneous and divisible structure of time in which consumer behaviour is set. In particular, current consumer models pay little attention to the phenomenological experience of both time and temporality. This has inevitably led to difficulties in understanding the role of time, as purchase and consumption events are much further apart than for most consumer goods and services.

The perception and experience of learning which has an established and verifiable goal draw attention to notions of time beyond normal temporal horizons. The expansion of everyday horizons to encompass the experience and the subsequent location of the **'encashment'** outside of this **'extended present'** (Nowonty 1988) identifies a need to understand the multi-faceted total social learning time environment. It is proposed that an understanding of the preferences and successes of learners in formal learning would offer an insight into both the phenomenology of the learner's own temporality and that embedded in the product or educational service being consumed. Further, there needs to be harmony between these temporalities for maximum utility to be gained from the transaction. Elsewhere Gibbs (1998) has shown that a phenomenological perspective of 'temporal consumption realities' within a time continuum can offer these insights. Slattery (1995) has made interesting observation of the notion of time in education which has familiar themes.

The above is based on a model of the experience of time where learning is depicted as an essentially temporal activity. To achieve this, distinctions were drawn between the everyday socialized future of our temporal environment and two qualitatively separate futures: the distant future and the personal historic future. Goals and outcomes located in these 'futures' require marketing interventions which initially bring them into the domain of the time capsule, where personal comparative assessment exists, and then impart to them a wave motion to bring them through the region of attention to the consumer's present.

This enframing of time in education is particularly well illustrated in the work of Hassen (2003), Clegg (2003) and Ylijoki and Mäntylä (2003), which give full play to the expression of the changes in temporality in an academic setting. They show the tensions in tempo and temporality of academic life brought about through policy changes, arguing that these changes are not the consequence of academic evaluation but of external policy impositions.

Existential trust

To go beyond the barriers of the socially constructed cocoon of time horizons – in particular, we are thinking of Giddens (1991) here but similar concepts have been articulated by others (see Gibbs 1998, for a review) – one needs to

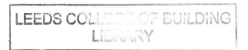

trust in unverifiable notions (Luhmann 1979). The marketing of education has to inspire trust to invest in teachers and their institutions to face a future as yet unknowable and even unarticulated (Bearden et al. 2001). This is no argument for blind faith, but for a form of existential trust which is built on humanity's potential for mutual respect, empathy and compassion. It requires our teachers and lecturers to evolve with students through a series of learning conversations. These might form the basis of a marketing proposition which can reach the parts that supporters of A levels would be embarrassed to have visited! If it is right to build relationships based on dignity, respect and personal responsibility rather than product-based transactions, then we might be able to embrace rather than reject those learners who do not fit the financially-driven strategies of our institutions and for whom our marketing fails.

Learner self-confidence

Self-trust is based on the notion of respect. It is the development of a responsibility for oneself as part of humanity: the realization of personal authority over what one trusts to be true. Such trust comes from the experience of involvement. If this involvement, whether in classics or in mechanical engineering, is to be more than a mere observational acquaintance with the subject, it requires the student to become one with his subject, so dissolving any subject/object divide. It requires the skills of rational argument as well as the passion of personal identification with the subject. The scholar becomes inseparable from his achievement. These acts of scholarship are acts of creativity, of becoming what one was not previously. They reveal understanding of the way we come to think of what we might be. In this, involvement is a condition of self-knowledge and conscious self-trust of a future identity.

We have resonance with the notion of self-trust, trusting in our potential to be, as Heidegger says, 'coming-towards oneself'. This is temporal realization of trust, for what one might grasp are opportunities revealed through self-trust, and the practices of trust, within the context of activities. It is within our care for what we might be. It is our concern for what we might be, in the context of what others will be, as a consequence of our realization. In this sense, it acts as a 'protocol' for practice within a specific context.

To trust in one's own judgement, to make decisions on one's own preferences and to accept the results as a reasoned scenario facilitates the ontological integration of authentic and autonomous actions. In building one's network of preferences and acceptances in the 'everyday-ness' of action, one first reveals oneself as a self-trusting and then as a trustworthy person. Thus one who is trustworthy must be able to distinguish between justified competence in certain arenas, whether propositional or of capacity, and where one is incompetent. Burstow (1983: 176) claims that 'authenticity requires him to learn so as to be able to accept what must be accepted, and – something Sartre also includes in his description of authenticity – to change what can be changed'.

Marketing ends and an education forever

The purposes of the application of forms of knowledge are, we think, very different for marketing and education unless the latter is entrapped by the temporality of the market. Comparing the marketing concept with liberal education, we suggest that the former is about predetermined ends achieved through the application of marketing skills and technologies. By contrast, liberal education is about the critical development into an educated person. It is about the process, not the end, and is distinct from the academically-accredited person whose goal is certification, not knowledge. The goal of accreditation is indeed similar to that of a marketing goal and this is rapidly replacing the idea of an educated populace.

This debate about the temporality of the market has, to some extent, been rehearsed in the social marketing literature. There, Peattie and Peattie have developed the argument that we need 'a more thoughtful and selective application' (2003: 387) of marketing principles. They are not alone in taking this position. For example Gibbs (2002), Janic and Zabber (2002), Wasmer et al. (1997) and Brownlie and Saren (1992), who state that there has always been a paradox that 'marketing techniques are used by firms as much to influence and manipulate consumer demand as to identify and anticipate it', have all supported the view that the ideology of marketing, built in the commercial era of the 1980s, is problematic when applied to other areas of human endeavour where the market might not always hold sway.

It is these views, at least for us, that beg a theoretical underpinning for the application of **techne** into the productive *praxis* of educational marketing.

The state which precedes *praxis* is **phronesis** – practical activity to further our temporal being – and it is a goal of education. It is developed through reflection on one's own behaviour and is different from reflection on oneself as a skilled agent in a range of competencies appropriate for a defined role in society. Reflection in *praxis* is not remedial in the sense of achieving some 'given' ideal; rather, it is iterative, an engagement with oneself with others. Existential reflection is not contemplatively dwelling on what might have been a futile attempt to match what we are with the totality of what others might expect one to be. It is a learning exploration and is a process of evaluating one's future possibilities for being, given the reality of one's current existence. It is the realization of what one is, and the diagnostic consideration of the activities necessary to secure what one might be, and it transcends self.

Summary

Without *praxis* informed by *phronesis*, our actions risk unquestioned inauthenticity. This may be brought about by the ritual and tradition of our immanent state. The market's dominance creates the institution's desired result of loyal customers – perhaps through repeat mailings to alumni. This closes off future possibilities, hinging them to the temporality of linearity and rationality (Habermas 1998), a rationality of the social present, of bad faith and of inauthenticity. Encouraged by the desire to satisfy the owners of the means of education, for example, governments and rich donors, marketing activities become guided by the instrumentality of *techne*. This has been proven successful in other spheres of consumption but, thoughtlessly adopted, commoditizes education in the process. Marketing *per se* is not to blame for this enframing of education – this is being forced by policy-makers, and those they have empowered, by means developed for commercial exploitation – but it is inappropriate for education's intrinsic worth. If we continue to market education through the ways of consumerism, education will lose its transcendental potential and adopt the functionality of the market. What seems ironic is that, in securing resources for education, marketing changes the educational essence of what it was intended to liberate.

4 'The student as customer' perspective

The emergence of marketing in higher education has been greeted with mixed responses. On the one hand, there are those who have embraced the idea wholeheartedly, seeing it not just as a key aspect for twenty-first-century higher education management, but also and even more importantly as an inevitable response to the overarching forces that have necessitated its role and place in higher education (Smith et al. 1995). Critics of marketing in education and higher education in particular have focused their arguments on the notion of what we could call an incompatibility theory, based on what they see as a clash of values between the world of business and the arena of education. The purpose of this chapter is to review the arguments and counter-arguments characterizing the emergence of the discourse and practice of marketing in higher education. In particular, the chapter examines the debates centred on the use of the customer label to identify students in higher education. To contextualize these debates we need to move backwards a little and first examine the forces that have driven the emergence of marketing in education and in higher education in particular.

What has driven the marketization of education?

Traditionally, education has been viewed as the means by which past and current wisdom is passed to future generations through instruction designed by teachers and for which students were to be eternally grateful. In that environment, the teacher possessed all the knowledge which students required to prepare them for life after school. Much has changed in our educational institutions, reflecting a significant shift from a highly inward-looking and teacher-centred educational landscape and provision to one that sees and acknowledges the role of students as partners and collaborators in the learning process. Despite these significant shifts, there remains a core of resistance that refuses to bring the world of business and its ideas into the educational arena.

The concept of marketing itself has a history, understood initially from a promotion and advertising perspective. Today, however, its meaning is more broad-based and about delivering value to those with whom the organization has a relationship. It is often the historical roots and understanding of marketing that shape the criticisms and arguments associated with its emergence in education.

Essentially, there are four overarching forces that have driven higher education to embrace the marketing idea (Smith et al. 1995) and these forces appear to have operated both in the higher education environments of developed and less developed countries (Maringe and Foskett 2002).

Massification of higher education

There have been three main waves that have characterized global educational expansion. The first was targeted at the elementary and primary levels. Fuelled by social justice, equality, equity and economic arguments and supported unequivocally by the World Bank and the International Monetary Fund (IMF) rhetoric, primary and elementary education became both universal and compulsory in many parts of the world. The growth at primary and elementary levels had to be reflected by corresponding expansion at secondary school levels. In many developed countries on both sides of the Atlantic, including the USA, the UK, Germany, France, Canada, Australia and Japan, the school-leaving age has been raised to 16, an age when most young people would have completed four or five years of secondary education. In some less developed countries, for example, Zimbabwe, South Africa and some South American nations, secondary schooling has largely been made accessible to all pupils. This in turn has led to the expansion of tertiary provision to cater for and absorb the rising demand from the secondary sector. Parallel developments, driven by philosophical repositioning of education as a lifelong process including the adoption of widening participation concepts, have also led to increased access to higher education across the world. The effects of **massification** of higher education on teaching, examination performance, physical facilities, institutional management, financing and student quality of life have thus become topical areas of research and debate in higher education across the world. How institutions, in this new environment, would continue to deliver value to students has thus become a core academic, management and administrative concern for contemporary higher education institutions.

Expansion and diversification

Related to massification are the concepts of expansion and diversification. As higher education provision became more broad-based, fuelled as it was by social justice, economic and equality motives, institutions have responded through diversifying their provision. Essentially diversification entails development of different types of higher education provision. For example, following devolution in 1992 in England, former polytechnic institutions which hitherto had specialized in vocational training became incorporated as universities in their own right. Since then they have grown and strengthened their vocational mission and proudly stand alongside traditional pre-1992 universities, offering a distinctive higher education experience highly sought after by a large group of students in society.

Growth in higher education has been phenomenal in many parts of the world over the past few decades. In 1963, at the time of the Robbins Report in England, there were about 324,000 students in higher education. The figure rose to 1.2 million in the early 1990s following devolution. Currently, it is estimated that there are about 1.8 million students in higher education in England (UKCOSA 2004). Thus UK higher education has been transformed from elite to a mass system with multi-level access points to a multi-discipline higher education experience. Subjects that would never have been dreamt of comprising a higher education experience a few hundred years ago, such as fashion, sports, music, drama and dance, are increasingly gaining a market share and have become the mainstay programmes for some universities in the higher education sector. This illustrates, in part, the nature and extent of diversity.

Nor has this expansion and diversity passed by the less developed countries. Zimbabwe, for example, was served by one university for more than three decades since the inception of the University of Zimbabwe, which catered for about 2000 students. The country has currently 12 universities which have emerged in the past ten years serving approximately 60,000 students in a range of subjects and new disciplines that have previously not featured in the higher education landscape. What has happened across many countries is the erosion of the traditional university, with places for society's highly talented select few, to a provision that is more broad-based and open to a wider range of talents and creating diverse opportunities and experiences for thousands of young people.

Essentially expansion and diversity have spurred on competition between institutions in the higher education sectors, directly resulting in expanded choices for students and also indirectly, by means of the strategic responses of institutions to become more focused on students' needs rather than institutional competences.

Growth of heterogeneity in higher education

Heterogeneity, the growth of diversity and difference, is a direct consequence of the above factors of massification and expansion in higher education. It is manifested in many ways but chiefly in the nature and composition of student bodies on campuses across the world, the wider range of higher education courses or products and, more prominently, in the academic content and delivery mechanisms.

Some would argue, and rightly, that the dynamics of student populations on university campuses are the direct result and consequence of the globalization phenomenon (Altbach and McGill Peterson 1999). Globalization, defined variously by different authors, is a concept that has attracted much attention and is sometimes considered to be at the heart of many changes that are shaping contemporary higher education landscapes. Essentially, it is a term used to describe the shrinking or diminishing of national boundaries due to advances in technology and the increasing economic and social interdependence of nations, with stronger links established especially between and among regional nations such as the European Union. Globalization has seen the demise of political boundaries and the promotion of co-operation among once different countries, frequently necessitating the 'free' movement of people across nations for socio-economic advancement, technological and educational purposes. As a consequence, students' options for higher education are no longer constrained by national boundaries. Rapid developments in Internet-based distance-learning, branch campuses and offshore learning opportunities, among other technology-led educational innovations such as **e-learning** and **m-learning**, have expanded opportunities for students to study outside their countries of origin.

The growing heterogeneity in higher education has ushered in a new outward-looking environment which is taking higher education out of its traditional comfort zone of being a 'sought-after good for society' to one requiring institutions to become more explicit in their marketing intentions and strategies. This looking outside rather than inside requires new understandings of the multicultural diversity characterizing higher education institutions today. In addition, this more diverse group of students has so much to choose from that institutions are, more than ever before, seeking ways of winning the competition for recruitment, curriculum development, teaching, assessment and learning support. In the final analysis, those institutions that do not have a distinctiveness desired by students and which offer no practical solutions to the needs of diverse scholars will have to be content with a life in the shadows of competitors or indeed face closure in the long term.

The growth of competition in higher education

The growth of competition in higher education has been both a result of and a response to the above factors. Equally, it has been a product of deliberate government policies in many countries, growing out of the sea change of global economies responding to the ideology of market forces (Altbach and McGill Peterson 1999). In Australia and New Zealand, countries among the forerunners in introducing marketing into higher education (Mazzarol et al. 2000), legislative pressure was placed on universities to embrace marketing as a key strategic aspect of institutional development. In England, the most celebrated attempt to bring full-blown internal markets in higher education was directed through the University Funding Council which encouraged universities to bid against each other for funded student places (Smith et al. 1995). Although this was directly and subtly rejected by universities, it nevertheless raised institutional consciousness about the 'inexorable growth of a competitive culture' (1995: 11) in higher education. The increase in university fees in the late 1980s in England, despite being primarily aimed at encouraging managed expansion, has led to a university system that is broadly market led.

More recently, the introduction of top-up fees and income contingent loans (ICL) has tightened the screws on the marketization of higher education in England. The result of all this is likely to be full-blown competition for students, research funding, resources and university teachers, and may result in an increasing tendency towards forming mergers between institutions in much the same way as happens in business especially during times of financial austerity.

In this highly marketized environment, the language of marketing has begun to have a stranglehold on the higher education environment. Given the centrality of the customer as the heart and soul of marketing, the question higher education has and continues to struggle with is whether we should view students as customers and academics as service providers. The debates have gone beyond the superficial levels relating to decisions about using labels from the business sector in higher education to more fundamental levels, reflecting a deep concern as to whether students in higher education should or could be equated to someone intending to make a purchase in a supermarket, for example. It is to this rather contentious issue that the chapter now turns.

Higher education: beyond the customer label and service provision

The debate around the use of the customer label for students in higher education is highly polarized. Coming as it does from the commercial sector, the word 'customer' is ordinarily used to describe someone who makes a purchase of goods or services from a provider. Students in higher education do not purchase education from the university in the same way. Although students could pay money for their education at university, they do not have the same rights and privileges commercial customers enjoy in the ordinary purchase process. They can still fail the course without recourse to compensation after paying money to receive a university education. They cannot return defective goods even if they are not completely satisfied with the products or services offered by the university. Although graduates are awarded certificates of their degree (a product), the more fundamental product of their relationship with the university is intangible, residing in their minds and sometimes in the form of skills that have limited application to very specific fields of human endeavour.

However, going beyond this line of argument, it could be asserted that students are probably much more than customers in a simple and direct purchase relationship with the university. Litten (1991) and Mintzberg (1996) have argued that university students typically wear four distinct hats, each characterizing a significant relationship they have with their institution during their period of study. When they make enquiries about enrolment, seek advice and guidance about course and subject choices, and when they receive tutorial guidance from their tutors, they are probably wearing the 'client' hat. As clients they are mostly on the receiving end. However, when they become critical of indifferent teaching, inadequate facilities or poor or unresponsive administrative service (Sharrock 2000) – in short, when their learning needs are not being adequately addressed – they wear their 'customer' hat and act in ways which seek to have greater customer satisfaction delivered. As citizens of their campuses – wearing their 'citizen' hats – students have rights and responsibilities, conducting themselves in ways which strive to strike a balance between enjoying their freedoms while ensuring that everyone else enjoys theirs.

Higher education students typically involve themselves in adult forms of living and university environments are generally designed to allow this to flourish. The final hat a student wears is as a 'subject' with certain obligations. As subjects, students experience various sanctions such as late library fines, re-writes for sloppy work and re-sits of examinations if they have not achieved success at the first attempt. Other commentators recognize that this list is by no means exhaustive. For example, students could be 'novices' when they are acquiring the habits and nuances of the profession; they could be 'investors' when they establish small businesses as part of their training or as individual entrepreneurs. As Scott (1999) suggests, 'Insisting on a single definition, market oriented or not, doesn't automatically enhance their educational experience'. Of greater significance to teachers is the need to understand which hat students may be wearing at various stages and episodes of their higher education experience as a basis for creating and developing appropriate relationships with them.

The greatest fear academics have about the use of the 'customer' label for students in higher education is the underpinning business belief that 'the customer is always right'. This belief has become the basis for the broadly successful 'customer care' business in the commercial world and has resulted in notions which underline the centrality of the customer in decisions, especially about quality. Gerson (1993) has argued that among the different views of quality that people may hold about a product or service, the most important is the view of customer. But, as critics suggest, students are not passive consumers of educational knowledge and understanding. They are in fact active producers of these commodities, using their minds to interpret and analyse issues and thus placing their own mark, personality and thought processes on the construction and reconstruction of ideas and new under-standings. Taking this argument further, unlike a shopping mall, there are gatekeepers of standards in universities who determine who qualifies to participate in higher education and ultimately who qualifies to be awarded a degree. One cannot study for a degree in medicine simply because one fancies doing it, as one might buy the latest fashion craze in shops if one has the means. Therefore universities and, indeed, the whole educational enter-prise stand for something more fundamental than seems to be suggested by the commercial labels of 'customers' and 'service providers'. They regulate, control and enter into relationships with students which go beyond an ordinary commercial purchase contract.

However, because students are required to pay fees in return for their education, the purchase metaphor is becoming more deeply entrenched in the higher education sector. Wherever higher education student fees have been introduced, be it Australia, Canada, the USA or New Zealand, there has been a notable increase in litigation cases where universities are taken to court by failing students. They usually argue their cases on the basis of poor teaching that fell far below their expectations.

Equally, universities and academics are not just in the business of providing services. Education is more fundamental than meeting customer wants and needs. Education attempts to bring customer and provider expectations and desires more closely together in ways which seek to promote the subject/discipline of study while empowering the students to take their places in society both competently and effectively.

Having said this, it must be made clear the argument goes beyond mere acceptance of labels within the university sector. Our stance is that students are more than customers in the commercial sense, in the same way as academics are much more than simple service providers. However, our underlying belief is that we should not 'throw out the baby with the bath water' simply because we find the labels inadequately explain the more complex relationships between higher education students and their teachers.

Rather, we should seek to draw useful lessons from a practice that has obviously yielded tremendous benefits in the business and commercial sectors.

How higher education could benefit from a customer perspective

The three fundamental freedoms of the university – (1) to teach what they want; (2) to whom they want; and (3) in the way they want – have constituted the key weaponry in the armoury of higher education institutions. They have used them as benchmarks for measuring progress and indeed estimating the extent of acceptable change in the sector. Anything that poses a threat to these fundamental values has often been seen as undesirable, alien and intrusive. Society has now changed. No longer are universities seen as the most powerful organizations in society. The corporate world has taken over and has begun to exert an influence on other forms of organizations in a way never before imagined. Higher education now finds itself in a situation where it increasingly has as much to learn from the outside world and indeed relies heavily on others to maintain its viability. One of the new lessons universities are learning from the business and commercial world today is how to develop a customer perspective.

There are four fundamental principles that could meaningfully be adopted by higher education which come from the customer perspective. Fundamentally, a customer perspective in an educational setting is one 'in which the interests and needs of students are central to the organization' (Gray 1991: 27). We must add that, in placing the needs of students at the centre, higher education institutions need to keep in perspective the needs and interests of other groups such as employers, government, alumni, parents and funding agencies, among others. The reality is that the needs of multiple groups of people and organizations may often be in conflict. Maintaining the correct balance in order to keep all customers satisfied becomes one of the biggest challenges of organizations. For example, a university may seek to develop an area of research involving the use of stem cells from human embryos. The perceived benefits to society of this type of research are well documented, however, sections of society may be opposed on moral grounds.

Similarly, sections of society may be opposed to the funding of university programmes by organizations perceived to be promoting unhealthy lifestyles, such as tobacco companies, and this could negatively impact on the progress of research in that area. In the area of funding, government may be keen to widen participation and provide financial incentives to universities which recruit from communities that do not have a tradition of higher education, including those with a history of social disadvantage. Universities may see this as an intrusion into their fundamental liberties of enrolling those students they consider most suited to, rather than those identified by government as needing, a higher education experience. Maintaining a balanced perspective of all these issues is probably one of the greatest management and leadership challenges facing universities today. A focus on the customer, challenging and contradictory as it may be, provides the platform for enhancing the corporate image and improving the service quality and performance of the organization.

Four broad principles provide a focus for developing a sound customer orientation in the university sector and these will be briefly outlined below.

1 They may not always be right, but understand where they are coming from

Students as customers are not always right. In fact, one of the main reasons they come to study is to discern what's right from what's wrong. A vice chancellor of a university in America was recently quoted suggesting that the purpose of a university education is not to prepare people for employment and jobs, but to help them find their moral compass. Implicit in this view is that education is about training people to know, understand and differentiate between what is right and what is wrong. Yes, students may not always be right, but equally they have rights and we need to have a firm grasp on a range of aspects about our customers. In higher education, such aspects about customers which we need to recognize are:

- Who these customers are, in terms of demography, geographical distribution and **psychographic** qualities. This is best achieved through segmentation research.
- What they like and dislike about the institution and its programmes. This will include changes they think need to be made, their needs and expectations both in the present and future.
- The knowledge and skills they expect to acquire through studying with the institution.
- The content. In very broad terms, what they expect to learn in the programme and how they expect to be taught (the learning/teaching and delivery modes).
- Their motives for studying with the institution.
- Their progression and post-qualification needs and expectations.

It is important to remember that universities cannot and should not pander to every student need and expectation, but should be aware of them all the same and do something about those with which they feel able to deal, in a way which demonstrates institutional sensitivity and responsiveness to customer needs. This aspect of managing customer expectations is the second principle to which we now turn.

2 Students' expectations and perceptions of service quality need to be managed

The above provides a broad framework for understanding customer expectations of the service quality of the institution. The institution must therefore have in place mechanisms for obtaining and capturing the above data in a way that renders it easy to analyse and to report to key institutional constituents.

A key to increasing focus at this stage on keeping the student at the centre would be to involve current and potential students in interpreting the data and exploring its possible implications. The institutional perspective needs to be spelt out clearly and issues have to be identified as either non-negotiable or negotiable as a basis for the development of learning and teaching contracts between academics and students. Examples of non-negotiable issues in many universities include the criteria and means of assessment, while teaching and delivery modes often have more room for negotiation and compromise between students' expectations and institutional realities.

Another aspect of management is to realize that expectations and needs are not static and so need to be reviewed periodically. The institution needs to put in place mechanisms for gathering data on an on-going basis and making the necessary adjustments, when feasible, over designated periods of time.

Broadly, management of student expectations requires the following:

- resources in the form of data capture and analysis software;
- human capability to manage the process on an ongoing basis;
- involvement of students to explore jointly and realistically the implications of the data;
- a realistic trade-off of quality expectations which incorporates the views of both groups, in a way that does not compromise the programme, course standards or reputation of the institution;
- establishing a mechanism for keeping key student and staff constituencies, including other interested groups, informed about the outcomes of the surveys and research.

Marketing has traditionally been associated with deceiving and tricking people into purchasing organizational products and services for the sole benefit of the organization. Traditionally, it has been viewed from a selling or promotion perspective and not as an organization-wide management philosophy (Foskett 1995). Within organizations, the selling and promotion perspective of marketing tends to have a greater visibility than the more fundamental philosophical perspective. This suggests that marketing is broadly viewed within organizations as an operational rather than as a strategic idea. As such, it tends to be associated with unethical business practice. Eminent writers in the business world such as Drucker (1954) have suggested that the customer is the 'be it all' of the organization: the start, the middle and the end of business. Thus, understanding the customer, their needs and wants, their perceptions and expectations of service and product quality and doing everything to match or exceed these expectations, is the true meaning of marketing; the entire business, as Drucker (1973) would say.

3 Student satisfaction should be at the heart of the educational delivery service

Students study at university for a variety of reasons, including a desire to gain qualifications, pursue a subject of their interest, prepare themselves for the world of work, and as preparation for academic and research careers in higher education, among others. They invest time, resources, effort and sometimes give up other life opportunities to pursue these goals. While most universities will deliver these expectations to the majority of students, there are those who fall by the wayside and fail to achieve their objectives. In addition, it is not just a question of delivering on the ultimate goals that is important for students. It is also about the means used to arrive at these goals. When students talk about their experience at university, rarely do they say 'I got the certificate I was looking for' or 'I got the job I wanted'. They talk either excitedly or indifferently about the total experience of having attended their study institution. Research (see Biggs 2003) suggests that university student satisfaction is more closely associated with issues of:

- teaching delivery and the enthusiasm of teachers;
- being exposed to a variety of teaching/learning styles;
- experiencing real-world examples and real-life situations as part of learning;
- enjoying their university learning and having fun at the same time;
- having the perception of being rigorously but fairly assessed ;
- the perception and experience of being valued and respected;
- a service delivery system which meets its contractual obligation, both efficiently and effectively;

- the utilization of assistive and appropriate technology.

Student satisfaction is basically the extent to which their expectations, in their raw or modified form, are either met or exceeded by the experience, product or service (Gerson 1993) provided by the university. It is therefore important for university staff to have a good understanding of these expectations, to actively design and create ways by which these expectations would be delivered and to determine the level of student satisfaction in these key areas as part of the course, programme or degree evaluation. A variety of techniques can be used to gather these types of data including question-naires, interviews, tutorials, discussion groups, focus groups, telephone interviews, drop-in sessions, suggestion boxes, customer advisory fora, cus-tomer councils and student representation in university committee struc-tures, among others. More importantly, however, it is vital to have a reporting strategy for the data gathered and analysed from these approaches. Departments should develop the habit of publishing a customer satisfaction index (CSI), a service quality measurement index (SQMI) or a service standards of performance index (SSPI) for their programmes, not just for members of staff, but also for students and other interested parties. Satisfied customers tell happy stories and become a part of the word of mouth (WOM) marketing network, the most powerful promotion tool for university recruit-ment and possibly also retention (Bennett 2005).

4 Research directions in the area of student as customer

Although a significant amount of research has been conducted on the notion of students as customers, there are many aspects we still do not quite know. These include:

- how attitudes among academics are changing in relation to the idea of student as customer;
- the nature of practice in universities relating to students as custom-ers;
- whether there exists a relationship between type of university and its marketing orientation;
- institutional barriers and affordances to developing a university marketing orientation;
- meta-analysis and evaluation of national student satisfaction sur-veys;
- exploration of the nature, value and impact of student satisfaction approaches in universities.

Marketing and the transformative nature of university learning

Contemporary belief is that university education is a transformative process (see, for example, Freire 1970; Habermas 1984; Cranton 1994; Mezirow 1997; Ball 1999; Moore 2005). How then does a customer perspective contribute to this transformation? Broadly, university missions have tended to highlight three areas – teaching, research and service to society – and often brand themselves as centres of excellence for these aspects.

Transformative education is one which has the following characteristics:

- seeks to liberate and empower the learner (Freirean liberation ideology);
- cherishes the value of sustainability, ecological literacy and social change (Moore 2005);
- seeks to develop learners into change agents (Mezirow 1997);
- utilizes cooperative and collaborative learning (Cranton 1994).

The focus in transformative learning shifts from the subject to the student. A subject focus of learning is most efficiently achieved through transmissive approaches, where the learner can be visualized as an empty vessel into which knowledge can be poured and stored for retrieval when needed, especially for assessment purposes. A focus on the student, however, radically shifts the emphasis. Suddenly we need to know more about the learner; about the prior knowledge they may have before we begin trading new forms of understanding; about how best they are predisposed to learning; and what constitutes an efficient learning environment. We educate them not to be carbon copies of their teachers, but so that they go away capable of solving their own peculiar problems with ease and facility. As leaders of tomorrow, we want them to become masters of change in a world that is ever changing and we want them to contribute towards a sustainable planet, both for themselves and for the benefit of future generations. Clearly the marketing philosophy resonates with all these ideas and it is our argument that when academics have been drawn to marketing as a process by which we deliver value to those we relate to, then we can contribute more meaningfully and effectively towards the transformative purposes of higher education.

Transformative education and learning is contemporary because it deals with the *status quo*, seeking to establish a new order of things. It is a type of learning and education which is aimed at making students agents of change for the betterment of society. Fundamentally, it requires that we understand where we are now before we can consider where we need to be. We call this understanding the context. For educators, this context includes and involves the students. Where they are may be signposted by their current levels of understanding. If we have to take them beyond this current level of understanding, known sometimes as their zones of proximal learning, then we need to decide what new knowledge is needed and the most appropriate way to reach that new level.

Summary

Yes, the labels 'customer' and 'service provider' may not currently sit well with the perceived values and ethos of higher education. Indeed, students are more than just customers and academics more than service providers. Yet higher education has much to learn from the customer perspective if it has to overcome its current challenges of enriching the student experience, developing more relevant and appropriate learning experiences, contributing towards the development of transformational educational experience in a rapidly transforming world and ultimately delivering value to the students. What's in a name, after all? The real benefit is in the ideas and, for us, developing an educating orientation for marketing is the way to go.

In what we have said, we want to confirm that 'closing the loop' based on feedback from students is not a fruitful approach for higher education. Such an approach considers university education as a closed system. This is counter to an open dialogue which encourages engagement and empathy for others' views. There is a responsibility upon the university to understand student needs and to be accountable for changing what is appropriate. However, this needs to reflect a culture of seeking betterment, not of bureaucratic completions and closure.

In the next chapter we address this issue of development and strategy for higher education institutions that want to retain a distinction among other resource-efficient organizations in the knowledge economy. We argue that such a distinction is essential to the provision of education if all those involved in the institution and for the society that sponsors the institution are to flourish. This is not just a polemic but an attempt to allow diversity in the potentially totalizing ideology of the market.

We seek to promote the virtue of education in ways that do not cause its disintegration into the commodities favoured by the market. We are not against such strategies, but see them as limiting for those institutions that want to stand out and offer education not only for its own sake, but to enrich society in ways other than the economic. These are the institutions whose mission it is to develop intrinsic as well as extrinsic value. We believe this is the university's role and have confidence that it is desired by most institutions. Moreover, we think those institutions that do not make it their mission may lose any competitive advantage a higher educational institution can have in a society ever more dominated by the notion of personal rather than public good.

5 Formulating strategies for success

'A generation gap is opening between a new breed of ambitious young career-minded academics who embrace a performance-management culture and their older peers who cling to traditional notions of autonomy, collegiality and scholarship.' This is a key message of this week's annual conference of the Society for Research into Higher Education in Brighton, where academics were due to discuss a series of research papers charting dramatic changes to academics' jobs and professional identity.

(Tysome 2006)

The marketing literature is replete with normative and positive theoretical and empirical research-based papers and articles dealing with various aspects and elements inherent in the processes of marketing strategy formulation and implementation. And marketing of higher education is costing a great deal. It is estimated that over 5 per cent of traditional universities' and over 20 per cent of with-profit institutions' revenues are spent on marketing. Marketing strategy is not a stand-alone endeavour. As has been shown, marketing strategy is an integral component of functional area strategies of the firm, e.g. marketing, finance, and human resources, designed and implemented in unison with other strategies of the firm, i.e. corporate, growth, competitive, global, and e-business strategies.

These strategies are translated into competition to win battles in marketplaces. Firms that achieve sustainable competitive advantage capitalize on other weapons in the strategy arsenal, including strategic synergy between marketing and other functional area and organizational strategies. We do not take this rather rough, crude approach.

Marketing in higher education is still a relatively underdeveloped concept. Its acknowledged significance in the face of new challenges has not yet become fully embedded within the strategic operations and vision of many higher education institutions, especially those of the less developed world (Maringe and Foskett 2002). The belief that marketing is about advertising and promotion remains dominant at key levels of university administration. Its role as a model for developing the products and services wanted and needed by university customers remains largely unrecognized in many higher education institutions. On the back of this pervasive, narrow view, higher education marketing is further threatened by failure to locate its core value of developing the curriculum in the broadest sense of education, preferring rather to be associated with either research or teaching. In addition, the failure to harness the idea of marketing and continued misuse of borrowed wisdom from the business sector poses yet another serious threat to its viability in the peculiar higher education environments of the world's universities. Inevitably, attitudes towards higher education marketing have remained negative, especially among academics. As long as higher education does not interrogate these issues, the prospects for success remain bleak.

Strategic educational marketing as a network of relationships

The economic transactional market model of education is not without its critics – see Lauder and Lauder (1999) and McMurty (1991) for an energetic and contentious argument based on contradictions. For example, 'It follows that to understand the one in terms of the principles of the other, as has increasingly occurred in the application of the market to public educational process, is absurd' (McMurty 1991: 216). It is based on poorly established principles of utilitarianism which dialectically metamorphose liberal educational values into those of the business and the market. This creates the impression that the market can explain the behaviour of learners, even though its successes with other types of consumers are not compelling. Indeed, Barrett warns us of the consequences of applying market technology for it creates 'the Cave of Escapism where the people are amidst shadows, illusions, fantasy, fakery, puffery and nullity, which they know is not reality, and which for that reason, they like; they are knowingly displaced from reality' (2000: 333).

Although not as anxious as Barrett, for our argument accepts the need to blend economic and human capital, we feel that the determinism conveyed by the market could deny free will and would have considerable implications for education's role in the realizations of individuals' well-being as responsible citizens. Moreover, the funding incentives are for institutions to chase income in competition, rather than in collaboration, with diverse suppliers of educational experiences and services. A dependence on satisfying economic worth is encouraged by government through funding mechanisms and is a feature of transactions, not relationships (see Tomer 1998: 215).

The Hayekian amorality of the transactional market makes its role questionable when applied to educational issues. The market generally assumes at least partially informed consumers to establish a notion of fairness. Where this condition is not met, because of structural influences or the competence of those involved, the market does little to rectify this and even runs the risk of exploiting rather than emancipating its customers. Meek points out that 'the privatization of the public sector relegates issues of equity and access to low priority' (2000: 27).

Such an environment assumes a learner to be an active and intentional individual whose role is as learner of educational experiences, not buyer of qualifications. This has implications for the form of market orientation that is best suited to education – transactional or relationship. Li and Nicholls (2000) offer criteria for appropriateness of the orientation based on two propositions of involvement and market efficiencies. Given that education is more than creating human capital, involving the development of critical reasoning and awareness, they suggest that relationship marketing is the more connected approach.

Educational institutions, relationship marketing suggests, bear a shared responsibility with their learners for the choices and transitions they make on behalf of their personal group identity. They form a network where institutional capabilities and resources are allocated with the purpose of performing better for the widest constitution of learners. This differs from any neo-liberal definitions of marketing in that learners' interests are satisfied even to the disadvantage, in the financial sense, of the institution in the interest of developing a notion of being that does not commoditize the essence of humanity.

The humanistic/systematic approach maintains that this shift should be considered for its implications for human experience and human character. The system, its products, and its practices should all work to advance the interests of human experience and human capital based on mutual trust. The responsibility for the initiation of the conversation is borne jointly by the student and the teacher, for both are in the process of inquiry and deliberation. The application of this alternative humanistic view has been hinted at in the marketing literature by, among others, Hirschman (1986), Kotler (1987) and in the educational context Liu (1998). In general, this view maintains that the consumer can be active in the marketing engagement, seeking more than consumption within the community of learners. This is clearly problematic in certain market transactions. The view also has the advantage of not assuming the customers are autonomous individuals when in reality they are agents of the community or peer group by which they define themselves (Bagozzi 2000; Holt 1997; and also see Muniz and O'Gunn's (2001) proposals on brand communities).

The dynamic of the field of higher education

The complexity of education product

In a general sense, higher education produces a complex notion of product (see Drummond 2004), blending education and developmental experiences for its students with a certain educational preparation for the larger society. In a specific sense, the producer is ambiguous. Students are simultaneously consumers of the education experience, both as intentional and contextual learners (Foxall 1998), a resource for the development of others and producers of their own learning. To understand consumption as an attribute of being, one needs an understanding of the collective notion of self, not just as the physical barriers of the individual. This notion of 'I' as 'we' has its philosophical heritage in the work of the existentialists, for example, Buber (1966), Heidegger (1962) and Sartre (1990). This shift has an important implication for encouraging learners disaffected by the experience and aspirant hype of education and its marketing, especially the marketing of the award degree with its heritage of educational experiences and the purpose attributed to it of gaining a job. If the two become divorced, these might both be better provided outside the university.

Furthermore, the assumption of an informed decision-maker is wrong. Maguire et al. (1999) highlight the difficulty this creates for the application of proactive marketing. The choice of further education institutions is often driven by spurious influences beyond their control which weaken the impact of their marketing initiatives.

The complicated social role of education institutions

The independence of faculties and the complex nature of their work make it difficult to add value through changes in practices, and often require significant investment of resources. This is evident in the distance learning, part-time participation and outreach programmes. Also, the internal structure of many institutions means it takes a long time for their core products to reflect the evolving structure of the industries they support. This is because they do not see themselves in the system, but rather in a parallel market. When the mission of the institution is out of line with its behaviour, something has to change if it is to become effective. We live in an educational environment of anti-intellectualism and suspicion of the motives of theorists questioning pragmatic competence and directing hostility towards established ideas. This is evident in the attitudes of our student customers and of the increasingly influential employers and their organizations. The tenet of superior financial performance as a primary goal of the organization within a market leads to consequences that can be detrimental to the individual and the nation. Any shift to learner-based funding has the potential to enhance the call for a system approach, but for this to work the funding must come unencumbered by economic imperatives.

The importance of financial performance in a diverse education system

The institution must shape a market offering that attracts investment and which comes from learner choice – tuition fees and funding council grants, research, donors and other sources. These funding sources are the institutions' key 'consumers'. They provide investment to the extent that they believe the institution is providing a product that suits their needs. To fail to recognize this creates competitive disadvantage and so risks the institution's future or, set against a background of increased performance designed to obscure real diversity, at least relegates it below the desire of the state to rank everything. This ranking of outcomes is intended to hold everyone accountable to the same standards. As Blake et al. have pointed out, 'This in turn entails the devaluing, and perhaps the eradication of what cannot be ranked' (1998: 2). Performance is demanded in some areas, but then criticized as indicating lower standards in others. The simplicity of managerial accountability has a powerful attraction worldwide, compared with the complexity of the educational project (Pounder 2000).

Competition and accountability

The assumed benefit of competition created by market forces is that these forces achieve functional diversity and programme choice. However, this has not tended to be the experience of higher education markets. Meek (2000) analyses the relationship between marketization of higher education and diversity and finds it easier to link marketization with an entrepreneurial university model (2000: 28). He points to the OECD's *Redefining Tertiary Education* report, claiming that this leans towards market control within the context of a broader framework. This leaves institutions with the task of diversifying for the benefit of a body of students which is no longer a homogenous post-school cohort. Of course, this is more difficult to achieve when institutions, driven by market forces, give higher priority to maintaining their short-term income than their long-term reputation (Williams 1997: 287). The forces of globalization also continue to influence the management of educational institutions, not least in the adoption of convergent management practices (Bottery 1999). Although encouraging best practice, they reduce the scope that national structures have for redressing the injustices they can create (see Kenway et al. 1993). Educational institutions have tended to seek approval and general support from larger communities by bringing culturalization or integration approaches. In particular, here we are thinking of the Bologna Declaration (2000).

Planning a measure of accountability is harder to justify than on the grounds of finance, but helps evaluate whether money spent on education creates a coherent, learner-focused system. Student experience, recruitment and economic success are easily measured without the need to invoke qualifications. The stakeholders to the higher education experience are able to determine what they need from the system and how the system ought to respond to them. Difficulties encountered by the institution in creating a credit transfer structure, for instance, are not implicit educational issues but institution protection practices encouraged by a market mentality. These create problems of credibility and veracity for the institution and also for marketing.

The CORD model for a university marketing strategy

The marketing strategy model we propose is built on the core values discussed above. The model manifests the premises of temporality, trust and self-confidence in four distinct principles that are translated into a range of separate but related activities. All are aimed at harnessing marketing and ensuring that it becomes part of the strategic planning process of universities.

Research undertaken by Maringe (2005a: 564–78) suggests that current university marketing lacks an appropriate contextualization; is poorly organized and co-ordinated; is largely responsive and not strategic; and its application lacks formal operational guidelines. The CORD model, standing for Contextualization, Organization and co-ordination, Research and Development, provides a framework for raising the profile, sharpening the strategic focus and for developing a home-grown educational marketing philosophy (see Figure 5.1).

Contextualization

Models cannot be universally applied and thus need to show sensitivity to context. Contextualizing marketing development helps to engender the feeling of a home-grown initiative while allowing users to develop a deeper

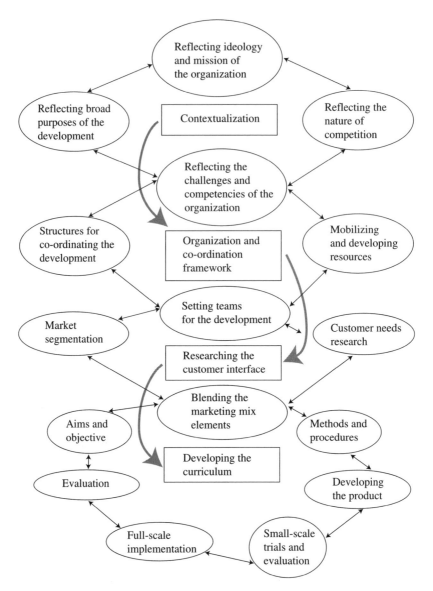

Figure 5.1 The CORD model of merketing strategy
Source: Maringe (2005a).

understanding and appreciation of the relevance of any proposed solutions. Four broad aspects have a direct relevance to this contextualization issue:

1   Reflecting the broad purposes of development

2   Reflecting the ideology and mission of the organization
3   Reflecting the challenges and competences of the organization
4   Reflecting the nature of competition

Reflecting the broad purposes of the development

Key questions that can be addressed here are:

- What is inadequate about the current situation?
- Why do we need to change?
- Why have we not changed before?
- Why should we be changing now?

Reflecting the ideology and mission of the organization

Walton's (2005) study of mission statements of top US and UK universities compared to corporate universities found that the creation of knowledge followed self-confirming statements of the nature of university. Although both corporate and traditional universities had a commitment to knowledge creation, the context of the meaning of knowledge was different and related to its utility. In the traditional universities, knowledge is concerned with adding to the stock of wisdom and entailed profound understanding, whereas in the corporate universities, knowledge is associated with knowledge transfer, training or more generally as an internal capability to serve a corporate objective. Walton does, however, wonder if there is a 'deliberate strategy by university decision makers to downplay, even to deny, the instrumental feature of their activities to the external world?' (2005: 18).

Walton's study does suggest that even in the top universities there is a notion of practicality in their engagement with students and other stakeholders. A review of mission statements of the top five universities (identified by having Nobel laureates on their staff over the past 30 years) suggests that there is a tension in the prioritization of the practical outcomes of education and the genuine desire to develop true wisdom. For instance, Cambridge University seeks to create a 'questioning spirit'; Harvard's education experience is intended to 'explore, to create, to challenge, and to lead'; at Princeton, the commitment is to research and to undergraduate teaching; and at Massachusetts Institute of Technology, the focus is on the development of 'the ability and passion to work wisely, creatively and effectively'. These missions mainly manifest themselves in enabling students to contribute directly to the economy of society, basically in finding jobs. For many, but not all, the presence of practicality within their mission is devoid of virtue; it is utilitarian in origin and lacks a relationship with others in the world. It is prudent and self-interested.

This notion of practicality permits developers a deeper and clearer sense of the institutional mission under the prevailing circumstances, thus providing opportunities for feedback to the overall institutional processes. It also increases a sense of belonging to the organization through a belief that they are contributing to its overall goals, thus bringing a sense of ownership to the developed curriculum. Key questions to guide reflection here could be:

- What is the institutional mission?
- In what ways does the envisaged development contribute to this mission?
- Does the current mission adequately reflect prevailing circumstances?

Reflecting the challenges and competences of the organization

The core business of any university and hence its greatest challenge is the development of its curriculum in the widest possible sense. All other challenges such as funding, resources and staffing emanate from this central mission of the university. Viewed this way, universities can align their marketing to reflect the core purpose that is the curriculum. Key questions to guide reflection at this level could be:

- What are the organizational strengths and weaknesses?
- What are the opportunities internally and externally that can be harnessed to enhance chances of success in the new development?
- How does the envisaged development address organizational needs?
- How does this development contribute to the core business of the university?

Reflecting the nature of competition

Marketing implies survival in a competitive environment and establishing the organization beyond the shadows of rival institutions. Key questions to aid reflection here include:

- Who has done what we intend doing?
- How successful have they been?
- What is the nature of demand for our development?

- How shall we differ from the competition?
- In what ways will our development be distinctive?

Organization and co-ordination framework

In order to strengthen the frail organizational framework for marketing that exists in many universities and to give the marketing function a more conspicuous presence than it currently possesses, three key aspects need addressing.

Structures for co-ordination and development

Most of the marketing activities of universities currently take place in disparate parts of the traditional departments. Without proper form and a discernible structure of their own, there is little hope that universities can pull them into a proper orientation. The creation of structures demands the definition of functions and roles, something which research has shown to be absent in many universities.

In addition, because research has also determined that current marketers work in isolation as experts in their various fields, it is proposed that the marketing effort be driven by teams. This would bring synergy and cross-fertilization of ideas to the higher education environment where interdisciplinary working is on the ascendancy due to the blurring of boundaries between subjects and disciplines. It is hoped that this will also encourage universities to address the current malpractice of delegating marketing responsibility to people without requisite marketing qualifications or expertise.

The development of structures also requires a marshalling of resources at the same time to support the marketing roles. The reliance on informal mechanisms for data gathering and obtaining marketing intelligence seen in universities is partly the result of inadequate resources in the marketing area. Parasuraman has indicated the need for proper marketing information systems which he defined as: 'Interacting structures of people, equipment and procedures designed to gather, sort, analyse, evaluate and distribute pertinent, timely and accurate information to decision makers' (1991: 144).

Researching the customer interface

If the core business of the university is the development of its curriculum, delivering an appropriate and relevant curriculum is the key to achieving customer satisfaction in the university sector. Researching the customer interface raises three fundamental questions. Who are the customers? Which customers are we going to serve, and why? How best can we meet the needs of these customers? These questions address three crucial issues of marketing research:

1   market segmentation;
2   customer needs research;
3   developing the curriculum.

Market segmentation

Segmentation is an activity that allows the accurate identification of needs in a selected group of the customer base. Degree courses in many universities are often developed on the basis of perceived rather than real needs. For example, at one university a BSc (Ed) is offered as a concurrent science and professional programme (BUSE 2006). More than 90 per cent of sixth form pupils interviewed in a Zimbabwean study indicated that they would prefer a programme which offered them choice between pursuing a professional or an academic route. Because the university had already decided and developed a concurrent programme, which reflects the product orientation of many university institutions, students were frequently told to accept what they were being provided or to look elsewhere. Application of market segmentation principles allows universities to more accurately identify the benefits that customers are really looking for so that needs can be more sensitively served.

Customer needs research

Customer needs research closes three gaps that normally exist between curriculum developers and their customers. The first is the gap between real and perceived needs. As experts we often assume that we understand the marketplace sufficiently and that we can design and develop curricula on that basis. Most universities studied work on perceived rather than real needs in the development of curricula. Consequently, a range of problems was noted, including inadequate enrolment in certain subject areas, students switching courses midstream, demonstrating against university administration and expressing a lack of satisfaction with current provision, and poor performance in some curriculum areas. The likelihood of acceptance and therefore institutionalization of programmes is increased when curricula are developed on the basis of real rather than perceived needs.

A second gap exists between the given and the received curriculum. Without a concerted effort to determine how the customers perceive the curriculum provision, there is always a danger that developers evaluate their efforts on the basis of what they believe the curriculum to be, and not what it is to the learners.

A third gap is what could be termed the quality gap. Often universities use internal mechanisms for evaluating the quality of provision. This includes various committees. Gerson (1993: 14) has, however, argued that 'the only view of quality that counts is that of the customer'. These gaps can only be meaningfully closed if the university invests resources and time into researching the customer interface. This also helps universities move from the pervasive inward-looking culture to a more responsive, sensitive and outward-looking perspective.

Developing the curriculum

The model proposed here is an adaptation of the Tyler Rationale (Tyler 1949) upon which most current curriculum development models are based. Tyler identifies four stages including identification of objectives; deciding on methods and procedures; implementing the curriculum; and evaluating it. The proposed model, by contrast, has two steps of small-scale trials and full-scale implementation before formal evaluation.

However, we retain the notion of market for strategic exploration for we live in a market economy and to ignore this would be foolish. In Part II we do not follow on with a discussion of the marketing mix, but develop our own version of what we call pro-educating. It is a concept which we believe has possibilities for a different way of delivering higher education's strategic goals of sustainability and contribution to society.

Part II

Putting marketing theory into practice

6 Positioning the institution in the market

In today's highly competitive higher education marketplace (Margison 2004), like all service organizations, universities have to justify their existence and stand out from the crowd, offering products and services in ways that make them distinct from other players.

The consequences of failing to position themselves successfully in the marketplace are wide-ranging and include operating in the shadow of other players, surviving on the edge of the market and, at worst, facing closure on account of non-viability. Market segmentation is a key strategy to positioning the institution which maximizes the competitive advantage of a university yet allows it to serve its markets in the most effective manner (Wilson and Gilligan 2002).

This chapter explores the idea of market segmentation and its application within the higher education context using both theoretical and empirical evidence to demonstrate its relevance to institutional positioning. It seeks to achieve three key objectives:

- to clarify the meaning of the concept by examining the way it is defined in the literature, exploring its broad rationale and illustrating how it is related to similar concepts such as targeting and positioning;
- to examine a range of market segmentation strategies that have direct relevance to the higher education sector;
- to review empirical evidence showing the application of a range of market segmentation strategies employed by educational institutions.

Positioning the university

The goal of market segmentation is to feed into the institutional positioning process. Hirsch (1976) has argued that higher education is a 'positional good' in which some institutions and their degrees offer better social status and lifetime opportunities than others in the eyes of students, parents and employers.

Studies which investigate factors associated with institutional or course choice by higher education students suggest that, among the many influencing factors, course and institutional reputation issues constitute the broad rationalization for enrolment decisions (James et al. 1999). Thus there is competition among producers and consumers in a positional market, where the former compete for the best students and the latter for the most preferred institutions.

Because no single institution can be excellent at everything, and no one institution can address the needs of all customer groups, new universities need to identify specific aspects around which they can position themselves in the market. Positioning is therefore an image creation process, aptly defined as 'the process of designing an image and value so that customers within the target segment understand what the company or brand stands for in relation to its competitors' (Wilson and Gilligan 2002: 302).

It involves at least three key stages: (1) the identification and development of the organizational brand – values, image and expectations associated with key products of the organization (Doyle 2002); (2) deciding on segments of the market upon which the organization should focus; and (3) implementing the positioning concept.

The UK higher education system is globally associated with the Oxbridge brand and this has helped place UK higher education among the most sought after in the world. The US brand leaders are Princeton, Harvard and Yale, which grew out of the Oxbridge tradition. In Australia, the Australian National, Melbourne and Sydney universities have ranked highest in the brand rankings and together provide the image and reputation that Australian higher education has on a global scale (US and World Report 2003).

The challenge for new institutions is that of fully understanding the global branding environment and then deciding how to fit and blend into this overall image. The starting point in this process is to identify the structure of the market and the positions currently held by competitors within the market.

Clarifying the terminological jungle surrounding the concept of segmentation

It is important to make clear the distinction between the seemingly similar concepts of segmentation, targeting and positioning. The ideas constitute part of a seamless process of strategic marketing. This is why the terms are sometimes used interchangeably, especially in everyday parlance. However, they occupy very distinct positions in the strategic marketing cycle and thus have specific meanings attached to them. These meanings are summarized in Figure 6.1, adapted from Wilson and Gilligan (2002) as a five-stage process within segmentation, targeting and positioning.

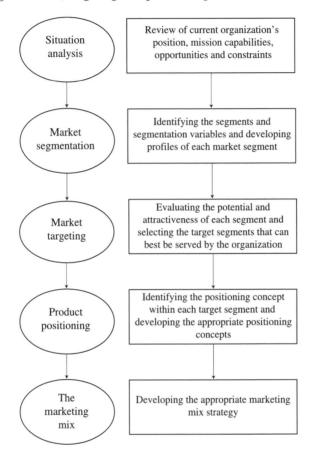

Figure 6.1 Stages in segmentation, targeting and positioning process
Source: Adapted from Wilson and Gilligan (2002).

The process begins with the identification of the organization's current position – capabilities, aims, opportunities and constraints – so as realistically to assess and analyse the institution's situation. This is followed by market segmentation, involving first and foremost the identification of segmentation variables, followed by developing profiles for each segment.

Market targeting is the third stage in the process which involves an evaluation of the potential for the organization to adequately serve the identified market segments. This includes decisions about feasibility, resource capability and ultimately profitability. Within each identified segment, the organization needs to identify a specific core product which acts as an axis for positioning the organization in the market.

Finally, the organization needs to develop an appropriate blend of suitable marketing elements as part of a strategy to communicate, promote and deliver the product or service in a way which results in desired customer satisfaction.

Market segmentation is thus an integral part of the process of positioning an organization within a market in a way which allows the organization to identify correctly those segments of the market to which it can most competently and satisfactorily deliver its services and products.

Although segmentation has its own strategies and approaches based on a variety of rationales and objectification, it is part of an organization's long-term strategy. This strategy is to increase competitiveness, enhance the profile and image of the institution, widen the market share and indeed 'raise the game' in a market where survival has ceased being merely a function of existence and become one of establishing a distinct uniqueness and character which meets or exceeds customer expectations and aspirations.

Market segmentation

Institutions seeking to undertake market segmentation and positioning strategies require a sound understanding of the nature of their market (Mazzarol 1999). The key to this understanding lies in undertaking market segmentation research. Although the concept has been defined variously over the past 20 years, essentially market segmentation makes a fundamental assumption that buyers or consumers within a specified market are not a homogeneous entity. They differ in many respects and some of these differences are great enough to warrant differentiated approaches in dealing with sub-groups within the market. A few definitions illustrating this key assumption have been sampled below.

Theodore Levitt (1974), reacting to the generic strategy of the 1980s which sought to expand markets through diversification, is largely credited with raising awareness about segmentation as both a cost-effective and resource-efficient strategy for dealing with expanding markets. He wrote:

> The marketer should stop thinking of his customers as part of some massively homogeneous market. He must start thinking of them as numerous small islands of distinctiveness, each of which requires its own unique strategies in product policy, in promotional strategy, in pricing, in distribution methods and in direct selling techniques.
>
> (Levitt 1974: 69)

This has the same direct relevance to higher education as it has to the business and industrial enterprise about which Levitt was writing. For example, three major distinct groupings have been identified for the undergraduate higher education sector for which differentiated marketing strategies are needed.

The largest group is the home students segment, which basically comprises local school-leaving students entering higher education for the first time. The second is the international student group, a fast-growing segment in many countries especially in the major economies of the first world. The USA, Canada, the UK, Australia and New Zealand are the major global importers of higher education students (Altbach and Knight 2006). A third major segment is the mature age student group comprising adult students coming to higher education not directly from school.

These three segments have widely different motivations for joining higher education, and may have incongruous expectations about the gains to be delivered to them through higher education. They also differ in many other ways including age, culture, ethnicity, gender and language which make them distinct individuals and groups within the higher education market. Thus differentiated marketing strategies will be required at various levels of their life cycles and experience of higher education.

Under this broad assumption about markets, segmentation has been defined as:

- the means of categorizing potential customers into like groups based on common characteristics;
- the grouping of customers and non-customers with similar characteristics – especially purchasing behaviour;
- the division of a market into different homogeneous groups of consumers.

Essentially, market segmentation is the process of dividing a large group of consumers into smaller groups within which broadly similar consumption patterns exist. The idea is to break down the heterogeneous market group of consumers into more strategically manageable parts which can be targeted and satisfied more precisely through appropriate manipulation of the elements of the marketing mix.

The purpose and value of market segmentation

Doyle (2002) has identified five broad reasons for market segmentation which we shall examine briefly in the context of higher education:

1 To meet consumer needs more precisely.

2　To increase profits.
3　To gain segment leadership.
4　To retain customers.
5　To develop focused marketing communications.

To meet consumer needs more precisely

In higher education, the demands and needs of adult and mature students are different from those of school leavers. For example, while adult and mature students may join higher education for purely instrumental reasons such as preparing themselves for promotion and more demanding roles in their workplace (Ivy 2002), a significant number of school leavers come to university primarily because they are expected to (Rodgers et al. 2001). The same curriculum, using similar delivery modes, may not have the same appeal to these contrasting groups of learners. What is needed is to develop distinct marketing mix strategies for each group specifically to address customer needs more accurately and appropriately.

To increase profits

The concept of profits is naturally associated with price especially in the business and commercial sense. The idea is to set the price of the service or good so that customers get their money's worth while the organization makes a profit (Drummond and Ensor 2003).

Consumers do not react uniformly to prices of services and goods. Some will be happy with low-priced goods and services. Others will only buy when the price is high, as this tends to be associated with higher quality, prestige and class. The development of the 'executive' MBA, which targets aspiring senior executives of companies and which is more highly priced than generic MBA degrees, has been developed on the understanding that there is a segment of consumers who will not mind paying a high price for that product (Everett and Armstrong 1993; Goldghein and Kane 1997).

A key to increasing profitability is therefore to understand the buying or purchasing behaviours of different segments of the market and to develop products and services that correspond to those behaviours.

To gain segment leadership

It is difficult for new entrants into a market to establish leadership immediately. Leadership in a market is often attributed to the brands which have dominant shares of the market and which are thus profitable to the organization. For example, retail grocery outlets in the UK are dominated by Tesco, Sainsbury and ASDA. Morrison's have recently joined the fray. Similarly the dominant brands of UK higher education are the universities of Oxford and Cambridge.

New players in a market can, however, take a dominant share of a particular market segment. For example, the Open University has a dominant presence in the adult and mature students market while others are establishing themselves as dominant players within specific groups of subject disciplines, e.g. Bindura University of Science Education (BUSE) (Maringe 2004).

To retain customers

Having identified the specific market segments an organization wishes to serve, the challenge is to retain the customers throughout their lives. However, their needs are dynamic. Following the experience of undergraduate study, a consumer's needs will change. It is thus important for the institution to invest time and resources into a continuous process of identification of new customer needs as they pass through different phases of their life cycles.

Post-graduate students have different needs from those of undergraduates. As post-graduates they may have their own families, have graduate loans to pay off and have more urgent employment needs. New experiences designed to meet these new needs thus become a prerequisite for retaining customers over longer periods. Thus a key aspect of segmentation is that of continuous identification of customer needs from pre-entry levels to the premium end of the market, as a strategy for developing enhanced products and services along the value chain (Drummond and Ensor 2003).

To develop focused marketing communications

The key to reaching customers is through use of appropriate communication channels. Not all customers have the same access, nor do they have the same preferences of communication channels. Female students are more likely to read a fashion magazine while their male counterparts surf the Internet. To target female students as a specific higher education segment, fashion magazines are likely to be the favoured communication channel rather than the computer. About ten million homes in the UK do not have access to digital TV. Communication messages aimed at disadvantaged students through the digital mode of TV transmission are unlikely to reach the intended audiences. Market segmentation thus helps institutions to identify appropriate communication needs and target media focused directly on specific consumer groups.

Approaches to segmenting markets

The starting point in undertaking market segmentation is to identify what may be called naturally occurring segments within the market, as discussed earlier in this chapter. Clearly, within these broad groupings of students are a variety of sub-groups or segments which can be drawn up by identifying factors which make them distinguishable and unique from the other segments. However, since segments can be drawn and defined upon multiple variables, it is important to bear in mind factors which affect the feasibility of segmentation. Wilson and Gilligan (2002) have identified six such factors which they insist should be considered when justifying attending to a specific market segment.

Segments worth pursuing in the market should be:

- *Measurable*: It should be possible to apply measurement to the variables of the segment. The criteria used to identify segments should thus be operational. This could include estimating statistical and demographical information about the segment in terms of population size and structure, the segment's attitudes to higher education, buying behaviour and anticipated benefits.
- *Accessible*: For a segment to be viable, there has to be established ways in which its members can be accessed, or at least there should be a viable plan for reaching them. In higher education there are well-known 'hard to reach' segments which have become the markets of choice for some universities. For example, traditionally, students from low socio-economic environments have been known to have a poor record of participation in higher education. Some institutions have taken it upon themselves to give priority consideration to these students in their enrolment policies. This has led to the development of tailored packages to meet the unique needs of these students.
- *Substantial*: This describes the question of size of the segment, which has to be considered in relative rather than absolute terms. The key consideration should therefore be whether there is sufficient justification for investing time and resources into developing products and services for the new market segment. Drummond and Ensor (2003: 45) argue that 'the group has to be large enough to provide a return on investment necessary to the organization'.

- *Unique*: The group should be different from any other in its response to a variety of issues, such as how it views the benefits or what it perceives to be the value of higher education, and sufficiently similar within its members in the way they respond to a particular marketing mix.
- *Appropriate*: The new segment should specifically be in tune with the organization's overall mission and goals and its resources. Anything which goes against the grain will require adjustment or overhaul of the institutional strategic focus.
- *Stable*: The buying behaviour of the segment should be reasonably stable, so as to be predictable over time. However, this should not ignore the fact that buying behaviour changes with time and that it has to be continuously monitored.

The bases for market segmentation

Essentially there are four broad categories into which segmentation strategies can be grouped. These are:

- geographic or geo-demographic;
- demographic;
- behavioural;
- psychographic.

We shall discuss these broad categories within the context of higher education and draw examples from higher education research. This will be followed by a more focused examination of specific strategies used to identify and determine market segments. In particular, we shall examine the use of conjoint analysis, correspondence analysis, profiling and cluster analysis as specific strategies that have been applied in the development and identification of market segments for the education sector.

It is important to note that no single basis for segmenting markets is ever adequate and this often results in incorrect marketing decisions as well as wasting resources (Wilson and Gilligan 2002).

Geo-demographic segmentation

The oldest and most frequently used method, geo-demographic segmentation, involves dividing markets into geographical zones such as countries, cities, regions and even postcode areas. Its essential purpose is to provide the base for targeting customers in particular areas who exhibit similar behavioural patterns.

In international higher education, the Asia Pacific region is known for its relative economic stability and growth potential and sends forth almost 50 per cent of the world's higher education migrants to different parts of the world. A key feature of geo-demographic segmentation is that it utilizes census enumeration district data (ED) as basic units for analysis and tries to investigate profiles of people within those sets and their behavioural or purchasing patterns.

Postcode addresses are perhaps the best known geo-demographic application. In higher education, the distribution of applicants' postcodes is used as evidence of fair admissions. For example, if the institution fails to show adequate evidence that it has recruited from postcodes associated with social disadvantage and deprivation, it might be assumed that its recruitment strategy was biased and possibly elitist. In the UK, two of the best known geo-demographic classification systems are ACORN (A Classification of Residential Neighbourhoods) and MOSAIC.

The ACORN classification identifies six major categories of consumers in the UK that can be used as a basis for targeting communication and marketing initiatives (CACI Ltd 1993).

MOSAIC is based on postcode analysis and has been used by organizations such as the LSC, UCAS and HESA. Farr (2003b) has redeveloped this classification system to reflect the specific needs of further education and higher education in England, Scotland and Northern Ireland by introducing non-census data which allowed a refined classification beyond postcode to incorporate household level data.

Overall, data based on MOSAIC classification system show that, while socio-economic status remains the best predictor for participation in further and higher education, other factors such as distance from home to institution, family experience of further and higher education and the pattern of choice of courses in different postcode locations have some impact on related decisions.

The large numbers of people belonging to these sub-groups within some postcode locations suggest that these groups constitute a critical mass for government strategic planning and funding focus. They also represent a target for the development of specific portfolios of courses in some institutions, including a refocusing of marketing activities and approaches (Farr 2003a).

For institutions which have an interest in international markets within the EU, a broad geo-demographic segmentation has been proposed by Vandermerwe and L'Huillier (1989) which identifies six groupings of Europeans based on demographic age, income, language, school-leaving age and geographic location. The classification shows that some potential consumers of higher education share common characteristics across Europe, making it possible for institutions to target relatively large geo-demographic segments that transcend national boundaries.

Demographic segmentation

Age, sex and family life cycle are considered to be the key variables in this type of segmentation. However, neither age nor sex alone is a good predictor of consumer behaviour in a variety of contexts. Nevertheless, there is growing evidence showing that women's and girls' participation in higher education is increasing at a faster rate than that of their male counterparts and that this could be associated with boys' reduced engagement, motivation, interest and performance at the lower levels of schooling (Barker 1997; McInnes 1998). This has implications for teaching and learning both at primary and secondary levels and at higher education level too, including the need to develop support strategies for the large but 'endangered' male segment of the learning population.

Choice in higher education is another aspect which continues to reflect gender bias, with the majority of female students opting for studies in the arts, humanities, fashion, music, dance and media while the science, mathematics and engineering fields remain male dominated (Foskett et al. 2004). However, applied science and medical fields such as medicine, pharmacology and oceanography are increasingly becoming favourite higher education study areas for female students.

While the majority of higher education learners are within the 18–24 years bracket, a greater focus is now being placed on the 25–35 years bracket for moral, political, economic and social justice reasons. Thus a new segment for higher education has been created for which new types of provision need to be developed, as the needs and characteristics of this group are bound to be different from the traditional school-leaving group.

The life cycle concept has become the most widely used variable for demography-based segmentation. It is based on the assumption that during the course of their lives, consumers are likely to pass through fairly predictable life phases and that these phases demand different purchasing behaviours.

For higher education, typical life cycle phases could include: young and single (majority of higher education students); young and married with or without children (majority of early post-graduate students); middle-aged with or without children (majority of late post-graduates, e.g. doctoral students); and older married/solitary retired (most part-time graduate or post-graduate students) (adapted from Murphy and Staples 1979). Some of these groups are more vulnerable than others and could be considered as disadvantaged and thus can be incorporated into an institutional strategy framework for widening participation within those segments. Other demographic variables often used to segment higher education groups are income and social class. Rose and O'Reilly (1999) have developed a seven-tier social class system, with higher managerial and professional occupations at the top and routine occupations at the bottom. However, income alone does not necessarily determine educational aspirations. A plumber may earn more money than a teacher, but children of teachers and other similar professionals tend to be more positively disposed towards engaging with higher education. Thus, as Drummond and Ensor (2003) have noted, social class and income are a less important predictor of behaviour in today's society than other methods of segmentation.

Geo-demographic and demographic bases of segmentation thus utilize characteristics of the consumer or the environment as a way of identifying market segments. They have been criticized for being imprecise predictors of segments, as people do not always fall into neat categories because of their outward characteristics, or indeed as a consequence of their neighbourhood. Better predictors of competent segmentation have been found to be based on the consumers' behaviour.

Behavioural segmentation

This comprises a wide range of behavioural measures including consumer attitudes, knowledge, benefits sought by the consumer, usage rates and response to a product. 'Benefits sought' is probably the most widely used framework for behavioural segmentation and is premised on the assumption that the key reason a consumer purchases a product or service is to provide solutions to their problems. These solutions are the intended benefits and they constitute the most appropriate bases for segmenting a market.

In a study of the impact of the new fees regime on students' attitudes to higher education conducted for the Higher Education Academy (Foskett et al. 2006), we found that potential students who were averse to debt could be separated into four groups. The majority were 'risk-based averse', that is they feared that going to university was a risk both in terms of financial disinvestment and in terms of there being no guarantee of employment to offset the financial investment. A second group comprised those we called 'sticker price risk averse' students. This group simply thinks that the new fees are too high and not affordable. A relatively smaller group was 'culturally debt averse'. It comprised students who just did not have a place for debt in their lives. Some sections of the Muslim community simply do not use credit cards and buy everything they own using cash. Their children therefore would not be expected to accept the new loan system which government was introducing to help students pay for their higher education. Finally, a small group of students would not get into debt just to experience a life of fun, amusement, debauchery, filth, drink and drugs with which they associated universities. We called this group, 'lifestyle debt averse' students. A 'one size fits all' appeal to these students to understand the benefits of the loan system to finance higher education would certainly be inadequate as it would fail to address the different needs of different segments of student debt aversion.

A survey in the USA found that there were several benefit segments in the market for MBA qualifications (Miaoulis and Kalfus 1983). For example, quality seekers were only interested in top ranked institutions for the prestige and opportunities for advancement that the quality MBA guaranteed in the market. By contrast, there are avoiders, who look for the MBA programme requiring the least effort to complete because they believe that all MBAs are the same. They tend to seek low cost programmes. Yet another group consists of convenience seekers who will join any MBA programme which is closest to where they live and at low cost.

Similar segments have been identified in Australia by Everett and Armstrong (1993) and Goldghein and Kane (1997). More recently, Ivy (2002), using correspondence analysis, has examined university image and MBA student recruitment in South Africa and found six distinct benefit segments:

- *Job markets* and *status seekers* tend to join the prestigious universities including those offering offshore programmes from the USA and the UK.
- *Business skills developers* tend to utilize the local technicon (equivalent of former polytechnics) institutions while *personal skills seekers* tend join the more flexible Open University programmes.
- Other segments included *network seekers*, who tended to join institutions with specific prominent academics, and *job promotion seekers* and career planners.

The adult learning market has recently been the subject of significant research in the UK. Based on the assumption that the market is not homogeneous, a recent study by Learndirect has been undertaken to identify attitudes to learning; perceived barriers to learning; attitudes to and past experiences of education; basic skills needed; experiences of learning post full-time education; likely future participation in learning; activities competing with individuals' time for learning; attitudes to different learning models; personality; lifestyles and media consumption.

Data obtained was subject to factor and cluster analysis, and resulted in the identification of segments of the adult learner sector. Seven segments were identified on the basis of their interest to learn including: (1) Personally disinterested and (2) switched off adults, who together comprised 32 per cent of the adult population. (3) Low priority, (4) independents and (5) conflicting priorities, making 33 per cent of the adult population. (6) Work motivated and (7) enthusiasts, who together comprised 35 per cent of the adult population.

Similarly, Graeves (2004) investigated young people of 15–24 years, their parents and employers to develop insights into their aspirations and attitudes towards higher education. Using cluster analysis and regression analysis, four broad customer segmentation clusters were identified while an aspiration index was constructed around six specific segments of adult learners.

The young people fell into the following segments:

- *Unfulfilled* (30 per cent) – comprising those low in motivation, carefree, unconfident but with potential, time limited and financially restrained.
- *Achieved* (34 per cent) – which included those who were ambitious, contented, below potential and those who regretted their past performance.
- *Disinterested* (20 per cent) – including the unconcerned, unconfident and the resigned.
- *Rejecters* (16 per cent) – including those who had some qualifications and those who had resigned.

The segments developed on the basis of aspirations comprised those who were:

- *Disinterested* (14 per cent) the majority of whom were male, across a spread of social classes.
- *Unfocused* (15 per cent) who felt they had little control over their futures and had no clear idea what they wanted to do, the majority of which belonged to the NEETS (not in education, employment or training) and to the older groups of the young people.
- *Dual focused* (20 per cent) showed signs of both high and low self-esteem and were likely to be studying in further education and more likely to be female, with a fair number of NEETS.
- *Community focused* (14 per cent) who felt they had control over their aspirations, are negative about themselves and not too optimistic about the future. The greater proportions were girls still in school and more likely to live in the South. They aspired to jobs in the social service and helping sector.
- *Disaffected* (11 per cent) comprised disillusioned young people who have rejected education and feel they are failures, disaffected about life and most likely to be still in school. The majority were likely to be boys.

- *Engaged achievers* (25 per cent) were optimistic high achievers, confident about their skills and are likely to be in university already. They aspire to professional and managerial jobs.

Research on student decision-making and attitudes towards higher education also provides broad groupings of young people who constitute legitimate segments that can be targeted using a variety of approaches. Adia (1996) investigated opinions, experiences and decision-making of students from a variety of ethnic backgrounds and found that different family settings had differentiated influence on choice and decisions about joining higher education. Families of different ethnic origins also had different perceived barriers to participating in higher education.

Roberts (1998), in a study of students' horizons, investigated student access to the Internet and the leisure pursuits and hobbies of young people. He found that these aspects were unevenly distributed across different groups and concluded that this would have implications for marketers in terms of promoting or enhancing services and facilities in their locality or campus.

Other key studies which shed light on issues of segmentation have been carried out by Foskett and Helmsley-Brown (2001) on perceptions of nursing and medical careers; Borden (1995) on student satisfaction and priorities with respect to quality and types of services, using this as basis for segmenting student markets within higher education; and Miller et al. (1990) on identifying benefits sought by a group of prospective college students from which higher education entrants could be segmented.

Behavioural segmentation probably provides the greatest promise for identifying specific segments that can be targeted both in terms of marketing and communicating messages for recruitment purposes, and more importantly for customer retention purposes.

Psychographic segmentation

While the behavioural base for segmentation highlights issues such as the benefits sought by customers, brand loyalty and perceptions of usefulness of the product, psychographic segmentation uses variables such as the activities of the applicants, their interests, opinions, attitudes and values. It is a lifestyles approach to differentiating educational markets. One such segmentation approach was used by Roberts (1999) in which he found that male applicants to university tend to use the Internet more than female applicants, who depend more on information in magazines. The implication of this was that in order to reach out to female applicants, the Internet would be a relatively ineffective medium of communication.

Psychographic segmentation stems from the early work of Reisman et al. (1950) which led to the identification of three distinct types of social characterization of people. They argued that societies are basically made up of three distinct types of social groups.

First are *the traditionalists*, who change little over time. Their behaviour, including purchasing and decision-making, can thus be fairly accurately predicted. In higher education, for example, because of the mileage they have over other groups both in terms of economic and political power, middle-class families tend to keep faith with the older universities which they believe offer the best opportunities for their children to occupy positions of power and influence in various sectors of the economy and public life.

The second group comprises *the other directed*, where individuals shift their thinking to fit in and adapt to the behaviour of the peer group. In a recent study of the decision-making of young people about post-16 options in West London, Lumby et al. (2004) found that a considerable group of 15-year-olds made decisions which reflected current fashionable trends as embodied in the lifestyles of peers and the new curriculum initiatives perceived to have relevance to a life in the limelight.

The third group, *the inner directed* segment, is a relatively smaller group of people who are seemingly indifferent to the behaviour of others and make decisions based on their own convictions.

From this apparently rudimentary classification of people's lifestyles, more complex frameworks have since been developed. The VALS framework, developed in the USA, has expanded the lifestyle classification system to nine segments (Wilson and Gilligan 2002).

The AIO framework, designed to measure Activities, Interests and Opinions, has devised two broad classifications for male and female life-styles, each with five distinct sub-groupings. The basic assumption behind these psychographic lifestyle classifications systems is that they portray something beyond a person's social class or personality – 'it attempts to profile a person's way of being and acting in the world' (Kotler 1998).

Research in education which has been based on psychographic analysis is sparse. Key studies are those of Roberts (1998) in which he surveyed the views of 18,000 sixth form pupils towards higher education including their hobbies, sporting activities and leisure interests. A significant finding was that going to the cinema was the top leisure activity for both boys and girls. The findings have implications on decisions about channels of communicating marketing messages to young people and for enhancing both recreational and educational support services for young people on campus.

The current university culture is characterized increasingly by a requirement to demonstrate a keen sense of competitiveness. A starting point for developing this is to have a full understanding of consumers' views of the institution's products and services. The answer lies in segmentation, a process through which the broad market is divided into smaller homogeneous groups with similar purchasing and behavioural characteristics. It becomes the basis for developing a sound institutional positioning strategy.

Decisions at many levels of university strategy require complete understanding of the institution's primary customer, the students. Quality provision is the key driver of competitiveness and, as Gerson (1993) has argued, the only view of quality that counts is that of the customer. From admissions and recruitment, through to teaching and training departments, accommodation, transport and services, widening participation and student retention, to recruiting in the international student markets, the development and delivery of quality rest first and foremost in understanding the needs of customers and then proceeding to satisfy those needs.

Analytical tools

Segmentation thus provides a mechanism for understanding the customer of higher education through a sound knowledge of their demographic and behavioural profiles, their personality and lifestyles (see National Student Survey in UK Universities 2005).

While the foregoing has offered a broad overview of strategies and bases for segmentation in the higher education markets, it is important to examine in slightly more detail some of the key approaches and analytical tools that have been used in defining and developing market segments in higher education. In particular, we shall review the rationale and application of the following analytical tools which are frequently used in market segmentation studies:

1 Factor analysis
2 Cluster analysis
3 Profiling
4 Regression analysis
5 Correspondence analysis
6 Conjoint analysis.

Factor analysis

In a sense, factor analysis is an umbrella term used to describe all the processes used to gain a better insight and understanding about given data sets which are presented in the form of discrete entities. For example, a survey seeking the reasons prospective students have for joining higher education may identify a long list of different reasons. The task then is to find whether the reasons given form some kind of pattern for certain groups of respondents.

Questions leading to such analysis could include: Do girls give the same reasons as boys? Does age of prospective students have anything to do with some responses? Do the reasons show a geographical pattern? Do any of the reasons given show positive correlation? Thus factor analysis is a group of techniques used to achieve two key purposes: data reduction and structural detection. Initially introduced by Thurstone (1931), factor analysis seeks to identify homogeneous subgroups within a population and so is an indispensable tool for market segmentation.

Cluster analysis

While factor analysis deals with individual variables and how they relate to other factors within a given range, cluster analysis goes a step further to investigate the relationship that may exist between groups of variables. The purpose again is similar to that achieved through factor analysis, that is, to reduce and interpret data. However, the unit for cluster analysis is no longer an individual variable but clusters of variables. Cluster analysis thus seeks to identify a set of groups which both minimize within-group variation while maximizing between-group variation.

For example, the LSC segmentation model for young adults identifies four broad segments: achieved; unfulfilled; disinterested; and rejecters. However, within each segment are a number of clusters which can be targeted separately. Among the unfulfilled segment are those who are carefree, financially restrained, with potential, low motivated and time limited. These clusters constitute sufficient numbers to warrant distinct and differentiated communication and marketing strategies and messages. The carefree cluster would benefit more from communication messages which emphasize seeing themselves in a new world while the unfulfilled with potential respond better to scare tactics which help them to move forward their potential to new levels of aspiration and achievement (Rawlinson 2005).

Profiling

Profiling is perhaps one of the most controversial techniques, developed as a data surveillance strategy aimed at using personal data systems in investigating and monitoring actions of one or more persons (Clarke 1993). It attempts to predict the propensity of individuals or groups to behave in a certain way through a careful analysis of a broad range of characteristics of the group as known from official data sets. For example, one of the most widely used profiles of mature students is that developed by Lynch (1997) which was based on four sets of data collected with the assistance of the Colleges and the Central Applications Office (CAO) and Central Admissions Services (CAS). The profiles were developed on the basis of the following:

- status, gender and colleges attended (the majority are part-time in further education and male);
- age (the majority are between 23 and 35 years);
- route of entry (the majority had a school-leaving certificate);
- socio-economic status (the majority came from intermediate non-manual occupations);
- domicile (the majority are found in urban settings);
- motivations for entering higher education. Four sub-groupings exist: second chance students; update re-entries; work-related learners; personal fulfilment (the majority belong to the work-related group).

From this, Lynch has profiled a typical mature student in higher education as most likely to have the following characteristics:

- a person (often male) under 35 years of age;
- has completed a school-leaving certificate;
- lives in an urban setting;
- most likely to come from lower middle-class background;
- studies part-time rather than full-time in further education rather than university;
- likely to be pursuing an employment-related course.

Davies (2004) has also developed a customer profile based on postcode mapping using MOSAIC to compare actual participation, retention, achievement, etc. with predicted national averages. For the UK, Davies has identified 11 main groups of customers to higher education based on postcode data. This profiling of higher education customers, he argues, helps institutions to identify best prospect postcodes for direct mailing and contributes to widening participation and more efficient targeting.

Such profiles enable fairly accurate predictions to be made about individuals sharing similar or dissimilar characteristics. They also have implications over a broad range of issues including the identification of equal opportunities, participation rates among different socio-economic groups and barriers to participation for different categories of people.

Profiling thus utilizes data systems which the organization may already hold or which may be held by other organizations to facilitate data concentration or matching. It has the long-term aim of predicting purchase behaviour of various segments and more accurately to target marketing and communication messages to appropriate groups and individuals. Its most significant application has been the use of direct mailing to groups and individuals who are assumed to exhibit the profile of the intended market.

Regression analysis

Regression analysis is a statistical tool for the investigation of relationships between variables. Often we wish to determine whether there is a causal relationship between variables or simply to determine the strength of relationship between and among a given set of variables. Where a strong relationship is found, it may be possible to assume that the presence of one variable could suggest the simultaneous presence of the other.

We might want to discover and quantify factors that determine the decision to join higher education among adult learners. Myriad factors could include occupation and earnings, gender, age, experience, previous educational attainment, motivation, and so on. Regression analysis allows us to determine the relative influence of a range of factors on a dependent variable to be determined, in this case, the decision to join higher education. Knowledge of the relative influence of factors can be an invaluable tool for marketers' decision-making. Equally, regression analysis can enable us to understand the relative influence of different factors among different segments of the market.

When the analysis is based on the relationship of only two factors, simple regression analysis techniques are applied. When it involves a range of factors, then multiple regression techniques are applied. In both cases, the starting point is to plot data obtained on the variables on a two-dimensional scatter diagram in order to determine the nature of relationship between the variables. Thereafter, appropriate statistical formulae can be applied to determine the strength and relative influence of the range of factors.

Correspondence analysis

Correspondence analysis is a set of techniques aimed at the visual representation of comparative data resulting in the grouping of data categories for ease of display and interpretation. It is thus a descriptive and exploratory technique to analyse data in tabulated form providing information similar to that obtained using factor analysis.

Ivy (2002) used this technique to provide a perceptual mapping showing the positioning of South African business schools. Based on 22 attributes, the mean scores of business schools' attributes were compared with the mean scores of the importance ratings to determine whether the aspects of business school offerings were being met. The same attributes were then rated by respondents in terms of the importance the attributes had on the selection of a business school at which to register for the MBA degree. Six factors, in order of importance, were identified as exerting significant influence on business school selection. These were:

- reputation and recognition
- academic quality
- academic standards
- views of current students and MBA graduates
- value (relative to costs)
- physical facilities.

Correspondence analysis thus provides answers to those seeking to understand the preferences in choice made by certain segments of the market. It is possible therefore to use correspondence analysis to identify which institutions are favoured by those who consider reputation and recognition as the key consideration in their decision to apply to an institution. Similarly, institutions can work backwards from these data to decide which of those aspects they would like to project more prominently as part of their positioning strategy.

Conjoint analysis

Conjoint analysis is a tool that allows a subset of possible combinations of product features to be used to determine the relative importance of each feature in the purchasing decision.

The product has to be viewed as a combination of attributes which consumers consider either in isolation or in conjunction with each other to make a purchase decision. The goal of conjoint analysis is to assign specific values to the range of options available to a consumer when making a purchase decision. For example, a student might be involved in making a decision about which university to apply to. Among a range of factors they may consider, some will be more important than others and the ultimate choice often reflects a trade-off between factors. Typically, therefore, conjoint analysis enables us to identify the major factors that influence choice and preferences, the relative importance attached to those preferences and whether there may be groups of consumers for whom different factors were more important (Soutar and Turner 2002).

In a study of Western Australian school-leavers' university preferences, Soutar and Turner found that the most important determinants of university preferences were course suitability, academic reputation, job prospects and teaching quality. Conjoint analysis provides accurate insights into students' decision-making and the attributes that are more likely to create positive preferences, while giving insights into the presence of groups needing specific targeting. It is indeed, as the DSS research on choice modelling argues, one of the best methods for measuring benefits sought by buyers.

Understanding what people most value in an institution's products or services allows the institution to develop strategies to communicate those benefits and to even redesign existing products or even create new ones with these in mind.

Today we no longer need to perform the daunting statistical analyses on our own. There is a good range of organizations which can do such kinds of statistical analyses using a variety of computer software packages. The majority of the analyses described here can be performed by a good SPSS package although there are numerous second generation software packages designed for specific types of analyses. The task for the institution is to decide which data they want. How and in what quantities the data should be collected are decisions that are more usefully made jointly with software and analysis consultants.

Summary

Higher education has become big business characterized by increasing competition in the marketplace. New entrants into this fiercely contested marketplace face many challenges, not least of which is the need to position their products in a market that prides itself on excellence in everything it does.

The challenge for new universities is how to become excellent and at the same time also different. What this chapter has done is to show that strategic positioning is best achieved when the institution has a good understanding of the market that it wishes to serve. Segmentation is a process that delivers such an understanding of the intended markets.

This chapter has explored the meanings and purposes associated with segmentation. It has shown that, because universities are primarily about students, investing time and resources in understanding their needs is the starting point for developing products that will satisfy them.

When we understand where our students come from, what their characteristics are, how they behave towards given stimuli and the general patterns of their lifestyles and life cycles, we can claim to have unearthed the geographic, geo-demographic, behavioural and psychographic basis for segmenting markets. This enables new entrants into a market to decide which markets to target and serve.

It is only when we have a good idea of who we want to serve and why we want to serve them that we can begin to create space for ourselves in the competitive higher education marketplace and thus position ourselves strongly through making product and service offerings that the customers are looking for.

7 The internationalization of higher education

Internationalization of higher education has become a global phenomenon and is gradually becoming an integral part of the broader strategic intention of many universities across the world (Ayoubi and Massoud 2007). The marketing focus of educational establishments has thus become more international due to an increasing interest in recruiting overseas students and a desire to increase global competitiveness. Despite the flurry of activity in this dimension of university strategic development, there is a lack of consensus about the meaning of the term internationalization (Knight 2003). In addition, the lack of substantial research which generates theoretical constructs in this area places internationalization issues on the periphery of recognized educational disciplines. Consequently, there is diversity in the nature of internationalization activities across different universities which reflect unevenness in the understanding attached to the concept.

This chapter has three fundamental aims:

- to explore the understandings attached to the idea of internationalization including the variety of adoption models in different universities;
- to review available empirical evidence in the internationalization of higher education with a view to identifying key advances and drawbacks encountered on the back of the internationalization agenda;
- to summarize the opportunities and threats to internationalization at both global and institutional levels.

The multiple meanings of internationalization

Universities have always been international in outlook. The word university itself subsumes a notion of the universe, a place where scholars generate and develop knowledge and understanding about the world both as individuals and as communities of people with similar interests. However, globalization, the process and state of interdependence between nations resulting in the increased movement of goods, services, people and ideas around the world, is often associated with the emergence of the idea of internationalization in higher education (UNESCO 1998).

One of the most widely used definitions of internationalization is offered by Knight and de Wit who define the concept as: 'the process of integrating an international/intercultural dimension into the teaching, research and service functions of the institution' (Knight and de Wit 1995: 8).

Far from being an event or an addendum of isolated activities subservient to mainstream university processes, internationalization seeks to embed an international dimension to learning and teaching, research and service into the culture and ethos of the university. It is a process aimed at fundamentally transforming the tripartite mission of the university as a place for teaching, research and service to society. It seeks to reduce but not to completely eliminate the parochial nature of institutions from being locally focused to becoming globally oriented. The link between local and international should always remain in sharp focus as the international environment always includes the local environment.

Beyond this generally accepted view of internationalization is the focus on the purposes of internationalization as a means to providing quality educational experiences, restructuring and upgrading the higher education systems and services. Focusing on the restructuring required as a response to globalization forces, van der Wende (1997: 19) offers this definition: 'any systematic sustained effort aimed at making higher education responsive to the requirements and challenges related to globalization of societies, economy and labour markets'.

In this context, internationalization is seen not just as a focus or aim, but as a key resource and strategy for developing higher education in line with international educational, social, economic and cultural developments and a resource for responding to global imperatives and developments.

The above demonstrates two broad perspectives associated with the concept of internationalization of higher education, i.e. as a process of responding to the forces of globalization and also as a deliberate strategy to raise the quality of higher education provision to an increasingly mobile higher education student market. A key word search in journals of higher education and inspection of library shelves shows a variety of concepts and ideas that have a focus on internationalization. Substantial material exists for example on aspects such as:

- international education
- international co-operation
- trans-national education

- cross-border education
- borderless education
- globalization and higher education
- trade in higher education.

In many ways, these ideas have a common focus, i.e. in the 'de-parochialization' of higher education, but they frequently differ in their motivations and could be the result of a variety of economic, political and technological developments around the world. For example, while cross-border education deals mainly with the movement of students and staff across national boundaries, borderless education emphasizes the utilization of technology to reach people in all corners of the world. Thus, while the key driving force for cross-border education could be the need for intercultural learning and co-operation, the underlying rationale for cross-border education could in fact be the need to provide for unmet demand in emerging countries and economies in order to raise the stock of human capital across the world (Vincent-Lancrin 2004). We shall deal with some of these concepts later in the chapter as they represent a core of well-developed higher education internationalization strategies across many universities.

Globalization and internationalization of higher education

These two concepts are frequently confused and used interchangeably, because they share much in common, yet they are sufficiently different from one another to warrant some discussion. In its broadest form, globalization describes the social processes that transcend national boundaries as 'an economic process of integration between nations and regions ... which ultimately affects the flows of knowledge, people, values and ideas' (Yang 2002: 82), including technologies. The economic integration may be deliberate or spontaneous, but it is widely assumed that global market forces are uncontrollable (Cerny 2003; Yeatman 1993). Globalization thus entails the process and state of interdependence not limited or curtailed by geographical distance, 'a phenomenon in which the concepts of space and location are no longer constraining factors to either the process of production or the process of exchange' (UNESCO 2003). Most significantly, globalization exerts an overarching influence on social, cultural and political processes of countries. It is, as Altbach and Knight (2006) argue, a worldwide phenomenon pushing changes in the economic, political and social spheres and pressing human institutions, including those in education, to adopt an international focus and outlook.

Internationalization, on the other hand, shares many of the characteristics of globalization, but is more appropriately seen as a response to the globalization influences. Universities demonstrate an international character by exhibiting heightened visibility in most or all of the following:

- an explicit internationalization strategic intent with clearly defined purposes and strategies;
- an expanding and diversified staff and student international exchange programme;
- a strong presence in the international student recruitment market;
- a robust drive for exporting educational services beyond the campus boundaries especially to foreign and overseas destinations;
- a curriculum development focus that seeks to integrate an international dimension into course programmes, in teaching content and pedagogical approaches;
- development of research programmes that are deliberately international in focus, both in terms of international collaboration and in the international focus of the research intentions and purposes;
- joint research and development activities with international and global organizations.

Thus globalization provides the external environment of a rapidly integrating world economic order which is pushing universities to adopt internationalization ideologies, strategies and approaches. Globalization provides the push for universities to internationalize.

Drivers of internationalization

The single most important driver of internationalization is globalization. Therefore, as the globalization processes accelerate, so too will those of internationalization within universities. Driving this acceleration is a raft of forces which include:

- *The new knowledge society*: the perceived importance of knowledge production, dissemination, and application in a world rapidly changing socially, economically and culturally necessitates new forms of higher education which embed a pluralistic global outlook rather than a monolithic national perspective.
- *The ICT revolution*: the rapid growth of information and communication technologies and the Internet help to make knowledge transfer and application more speedy, reliable and efficient. New forms of teaching, learning and research can enhance the capacity of universities to adopt global perspectives for educational provision and curriculum.

- *A growing utilitarianism in higher education*: Madonna sang about being a material girl. The world has changed with her. There is a growing utilitarianism in education in which students study degree courses perceived to offer the greatest financial rewards in the world of work. The idea of education and knowledge for its own sake – the intrinsic value of learning – is becoming subordinate to the tangible benefits associated with engaging with higher education. Working for international organizations and in international contexts is certainly more appealing and rewarding for graduates. Consequently, universities are under pressure to prepare students for the world of work in the international context. Many universities are incorporating a strong business orientation, work-based learning approaches, international work and study experience as strategies to prepare their graduates for work in the international context.
- *Growing demand for higher education*: the demand for higher education is growing globally. In some countries such as the UK, this demand is fuelled by deliberate widening participation policies which set targets for 50 per cent participation in higher education of the 18–30-year-old population. In many developing countries, supply continues to fail to meet demand. Zimbabwe, for example, has 12 universities with a combined annual intake capacity of under 50,000. However, there is an annual demand for university places in excess of 75,000 (Maringe 2004). Many of these students look outside the country to provide their higher education needs. Thus, a lack of capacity in many developing countries is helping fuel academic migration to the more developed world, creating a ready market for overseas institutions to recruit internationally.
- *Political and economic instability*: Africa and the Middle East are currently the world's hotspots of political and economic instability. In a study of the migration reasons of students studying in UK higher education, Maringe and Carter (2007) found that political and economic instability were considered the strongest push factors for deciding to study outside their home countries. Adoption of an international dimension thus becomes a necessary part of the strategic intention of many universities in this context.
- *Decreasing public funding of higher education*: Foskett et al. (2006) undertook a study for the Higher Education Academy on the impact of increased fees in higher education and found that raising university fees does not depress demand for places in any significant way especially if students have the option to study and pay later. As students begin to have a sense of sharing the financial costs of their higher education experience, so also do they more effectively commodify the higher education product experience and service. International students, who pay significantly higher

fees than home students, probably feel a greater need to see tangible evidence of the outcomes of their higher education experience. In addition to the general academic support offered to all students, many universities have specific international students' affairs offices and budgets. They organize many activities for international students aimed at enriching their higher education experience in full recognition of their greater needs for social and cultural integration and the greater investment they make to their university educational experience.

The above drivers are creating a new internationalizing dynamic at the institutional and national system levels of universities. However, because the net movement of students and staff tends to be from the less developed to the developed countries, this has tended to exacerbate the brain drain which represents significant economic losses to poor countries (UNECA 2000). This leaves universities in developing countries with skeletal staff, and helps to create negative perceptions of poor quality and inadequately resourced higher education provision, causing more and more students to seek university places in the developed world and in more economically stable countries.

Given the above as the key drivers, how do institutions rationalize the internationalization process at institutional levels?

The rationales for internationalization

Clearly, the multiple meanings associated with the concept of internationalization and the wide range of its drivers subsume a variety of undergirding rationales too. A range of rationales has been identified by several authors including Aigner et al. (1992), Scott (1992), Warner (1992), Davies (2004), Johnston and Edelstein (1993), Knight and de Wit (1995), Blumenthal et al. (1996) and Knight (1997). We summarize some of the key arguments below.

Promoting world peace rationale

At the end of the Cold War, the major economies of the world were keen to make rapid economic progress in order to make up for the destruction of basic infrastructures and to improve the lives of their people. The maintenance of world peace was seen as a precondition to this economic growth and universities were charged with the responsibility of being champions in the development of peace programmes. Aigner et al. (1992) argue that the development of curricula programmes and institutes of peace studies in universities across the world provides evidence for this development. The need for co-operation between nations is undoubtedly vital in the development of peace studies curricula just as it is in the development of curricula dealing with issues of global environment. The post-9/11 period has also witnessed a significant growth in Islamic and global terrorism studies in universities in many parts of the world as nations grapple to understand the causes of Islamic fundamentalism and global terrorism. The desire for peace and international security is a key driver for these new international curriculum developments in many parts of the world.

The economic rationale

This rationale operates at two levels: the national and institutional. At the national level, countries aim to create greater prosperity for their people and prepare them more adequately for opportunities in the international context. Nations also aspire to attract the best brains and skilled manpower from across the world to work in their countries. Universities are thus seen as the logical starting point for developing the corpus of manpower required for working in international environments. The more a nation's higher education system is perceived as offering an international dimension, the more it will attract people from abroad to its shores. Research has persistently shown that a nation's economic competitiveness is directly related to the quality of its higher education system. The USA, Japan, Australia, Canada, and the UK are dominant economic giants globally and their higher education systems are simultaneously perceived to be of high or very high quality internationally (Adams 2004). Overall, the following facts about the contribution that UK universities make to the national economy serve to show the importance of higher education to the economic well-being of nations.

- The total revenue from UK universities in 2003–2004 surpassed that of key economic players such as the pharmaceutical industries at approximately £17 billion.
- Universities employ approximately 1.2 per cent of total UK employment.
- For every 100 jobs within UK universities, a further 99 are created in the economy.
- International students contribute approximately 10 per cent of all UK receipts from overseas visitors.
- International students' expenditure generates about £2.4 billion output across the economy and over 21,900 jobs.

These facts are summarized from research conducted on behalf of Universities UK by the University of Strathclyde in 2003–2004 which has led to the following conclusion about the impact of universities on the national economy: 'Higher education institutions are independent business entities and the economic activity generated by institutional expenditure, an activity most readily quantifiable, is substantial' (Universities UK 2004/05: 6).

In line with this overall assessment, the White Paper *The Future of Higher Education* (DfES 2003) and the Lambert Review of university/business collaboration (2003) have also concluded that the higher education sector plays a pivotal role in ensuring the country's economic competitiveness.

The economic competitiveness of individual institutions is measured in a variety of ways such as the diversity of their income base, their annual financial turnover, their contribution to regional and national economic development, the diversity of their employment profiles and their attraction for foreign students and staff, among other factors. Universities with a demonstrably strong international focus tend to score highly on these measures.

For example, findings from a study of the impact of universities on regional economies (Adams 2004) suggest that universities with the strongest international activity (located mainly in London, the East and South-East regions) have the highest number of research active staff, the highest research grant and contract income, the highest industrial research contract income, the highest PhD awards, and the most published research papers. In addition, these three regions account for 60 per cent of money jointly spent on research and development by university/business collaborations. In terms of the nature of economic activity, universities in these regions tend to focus their research and development efforts on key economic activities in the pharmaceutical, biotechnology, communications and IT areas, activities indicated as the key to global economic competitiveness of nations. There is thus a clear case for developing an international focus as a strategy for raising the economic competitiveness at both the national and institutional levels.

The political rationale

Again, this rationale operates at two principal levels. At the national level, countries are keen to establish their presence on the international scene and, in so doing, exert political influence aimed at creating and developing a variety of societal values such as peace, stability, economic and ideological capital (Qiang 2003). In the Foreword to the government White Paper, *The Future of Higher Education* (DfES 2003), then Secretary for Education Charles Clarke noted: 'British universities are a great success story. Over the last 30 years some of the finest brains in the world have pushed the boundaries of knowledge, science and understanding.'

Demonstrating the central importance of universities in meeting challenges at both the national and world stage, he went on to say:

> Our national ability to master that process of change and not be
> ground down by it depends critically upon our universities. Our
> future success depends upon mobilising even more effectively the
> imagination, creativity, skills and talents of all our people. And it
> depends on using that knowledge and understanding to build
> economic strength and social harmony.
>
> (DfES 2003)

Since the period of empire, higher education and education in general have always been seen as modernizing influences and were a key part of the foreign policy agendas of Western nations seeking to expand their spheres of influence in different parts of the world. The creation of an educated elite in the former colonies was seen as an integral part of the political process of domination and economic expansion. However, Knight (1997) has noted that with the decline of empire and the establishment of independence in former colonies, this political dimension of international education has been reduced in importance. Despite this decline, the differentials existing in the resource base and economic advantage of nations, including the political instability this helps to create in former colonies, have combined to strengthen the belief that Western models of higher education are superior to those of the rest of the world.

This has helped fuel massive educational migration from developing countries to the more developed nations of the West. In their study of migration motives of international students from developing countries to the UK, Maringe and Carter (2007) identified the international nature of university provision as one of the key drivers of study migration. The colonial political domination experiment thus continues in a more subtle form in the post colonial era. For example, the Commonwealth is sometimes seen as a strategy for maintaining the previous colonial heritage (Mugabe 2004) through the perpetuation of Western values among former colonies. Higher education is seen as a diplomatic investment in future political and economic relations as Knight (1997: 9) suggests:

> scholarships for foreign students who are seen as promising future
> leaders are considered to be effective way of developing an under-
> standing of and perhaps affinity for the sponsoring country. This
> affinity may prove to be beneficial in future years in terms of
> diplomatic or business relations.

Thus, if education has an inherent political influence, then developing an international dimension in the universities, mission widens the recruitment market and contributes to the global politicization process.

The academic rationale

Key academic arguments for internationalizing higher education are related to the fundamental aims and purposes of higher education and to issues of quality of its provision. This rationale emphasizes both the responsive and proactive aspects of internationalization of higher education. There is recognition that current university learning spaces are populated by multicultural groups of students from a variety of countries. This calls for a variety of responses at both the institutional and individual teaching staff levels and the need to consider some of the following issues:

- Students from different parts of the world bring a rich cultural resource to the learning environments of universities. Internationalization of the university curriculum helps to expand the diverse sets of cultural capital and experiences, making these a part of the learning objectives.
- Internationalization of the curriculum goes beyond simply having students from abroad in the home university classrooms and laboratories. It seeks to engage and exploit the rich cultural diversity and embed it into the learning culture of the internationalized university.
- Internationalizing the university curriculum should go beyond tinkering with the content of instruction. It should involve a significant redesign of course units and programmes, including of course the content, but more importantly the teaching strategies and resources to reflect a more global perspective of university learning and to become more inclusive and truly international.
- Staff and student exchange programmes should be at the heart of the curriculum internationalization process. It is not enough for students to go abroad to study standard chemistry or history courses. Emphasis on these programmes should be placed on learning about diversity, through greater awareness of different cultures, traditions, lifestyles, religions and languages. When students return from these exchange programmes, there is need to deploy a learning cascading model which allows such students to share their experiences with the larger student body.

Knight (1999: 20) has argued that 'by internationalising the curriculum and enhancing the international dimension of teaching there is value added' in the form of, among others, enriched inter-cultural learning, multi-perspective learning and understanding of content, deeper conceptualization of ideas and greater acceptance of diversity. However, Bell (2004: 3) has identified what she describes as a 'spectrum of acceptances' of internationaliizing curriculum by university academics in Australian universities which identifies four levels of staff acceptance of the process of curriculum internationalization.

- Level One represents staff who consider the process as having a negative impact on the quality of university experience. These staff argued strongly that the university curriculum should remain Australian.
- Level Two consists of those who simply consider internationalization of the curriculum as inappropriate because it adds more content to an already crowded curriculum and because they consider the purpose of higher education as being that of preparing students for professions in the local environment.
- Level Three staff view internationalization as a possibility in the greater scheme of university developments while Level Four staff see it as an integral part of what they do. The pedagogical and content approaches these staff utilized were also found to be different.

The first two levels generally employed a content- and knowledge-driven approach to teaching with direct instruction as the key method of curriculum transmission. The third and fourth levels generally perceived teaching as learning-focused and learning as based on interaction and employing dialogic, discursive and inclusive approaches. The content of their courses reflected greater focus on international comparison, case study perspectives and deeply contextualized learning. Herein lies the value of internationalizing the university curriculum. Clearly, we can see a gradual progression from surface to deep learning as we move from locally focused curricula approaches to those that embed an international dimension. Thus, developing an international curriculum is increasingly seen as a quality mark of university educational provision.

The socio-cultural rationale

Nations across the world have become something of a cultural melting pot, with different nationalities and ethnic groups living and working side by side. Higher education learning spaces are pretty much the same. The demographics of working and learning spaces in contemporary societies have assumed heterogeneity of unprecedented proportions over the last decades. As we saw earlier, deep learning strategies tend to embed constructivist views and approaches (Dewey 1998). The importance of foregrounding the socio-cultural capital of learners, using it as a legitimate basis upon which new ideas can be developed, is at the heart of constructivist learning and results in deeper and more personalized understanding and reflection. This suggests that, in today's demographically diverse classrooms, students bring a richness of multiple languages, cultural beliefs and social interpretive analytical frameworks to their learning tasks. Apart from the academic affordances this brings, students have been found to develop a greater respect and awareness of the significance of other people's culture resulting in greater personal, group and inter-group tolerance. As Knight has argued:

> The acknowledgement of cultural and ethnic diversity within and between countries is considered as a strong rationale for the internationalization of a nation's education system. In addition, research suggests that a strong knowledge and skill base in intercultural relations and communication is considered by many academics as one of the strongest rationales for internationalizing the teaching/ learning experience of students in undergraduate and graduate programmes.
>
> (1997: 11)

A review of institutional internationalization strategy documents in 37 UK universities (Maringe 2007) has revealed a range of other specific rationales:

- prepare graduates who are internationally knowledgeable and inter-culturally proficient;
- maintain academic leadership in an increasingly competitive higher education environment;
- achieve and become recognized as institutions of the highest international standards;
- develop scholarship and expertise in issues affecting the interdependence of nations;
- develop and be seen as a leader in the export of educational services and products;
- work with increasing diversity and tap into its richness as basis for teaching, learning and research;
- generate revenue and increase funding diversity;
- contribute to global security and peace;
- promote intercultural understanding and learning;
- review critically the emerging internationalization strategies.

Below we have sampled a few of the common strategies used by many institutions to implement the processes of internationalization. For each of these, we review the overall strategic intent and highlight key barriers encountered by some institutions.

Student and staff exchange programmes

Literature identifies student and staff exchange as the dominant and arguably the most developed internationalization strategy (Huisman and van der

Wende 2004). A number of rationales have been identified which relate to this strategy, the most significant being to promote intercultural learning by exposing students and staff to other learning environments which enhance their understanding of educational and social issues; to help students and staff engage in the global circle of learning; to understand and appreciate other cultures and national traditions; to help create collaborative communities of learning and research; and to enhance the reputation of the university internationally.

In the UK, student exchange programmes have been arranged through long-standing programmes such as Erasmus Mundus and more recently through the World Universities Network (WUN) programme. The Erasmus Mundus programme is a co-operation and mobility programme in the field of higher education which promotes the European Union (EU) as a centre of excellence in learning around the world. It supports European top-quality master's courses and enhances the visibility and attractiveness of European higher education in Third World countries. It also provides EU-funded scholarships for third country nationals participating in these master's courses, as well as scholarships for EU nationals studying at partner universities throughout the world. The unique position of the UK-taught master's degree is that it takes one year to complete compared to two in other EU countries and in Australia and the USA.

However, with the proposed harmonization of higher education through the Bologna Protocol, under which it is anticipated that all master's degrees will be completed over two years, the competitive advantage of the UK provision is currently under serious threat. Further, as more and more universities in the EU are turning to the use of English as the medium of instruction, it is anticipated that future migration to the UK for study purposes will be significantly reduced. To date, the other barrier to student exchange programmes has been that of language, especially in some EU countries. Without a sound grasp of the language of the host country, many universities place restrictions on learning participation. In response to this, a number of universities have put in place pre-master's programmes which involve a combination of study skills, and English language enhancement skills for specific academic subject and study pathways. Currently, the expansion of such programmes is a key strategic issue of many universities in the UK.

The International Research Mobility Programme (IRMP) provides scholarships to facilitate staff and postgraduate student exchange between the WUN partner institutions. The aim of the scheme is to increase the opportunities for young researchers and post-graduate students to engage in international collaborative research and to experience different research environments. Within some institutions, the scheme also contributes to the development of networks and longer-term research links with WUN partners in the USA, China and Europe.

Curriculum internationalization

As pointed out earlier, the processes of internationalizing the university curriculum are varied and involve different levels of integration with existing practices. In many countries, internationalization of the curriculum falls within a broader remit of university curriculum reform. For example, in Japan and Denmark, there is a growing social demand for education that prepares students for careers and lives in a global society (Boegh and Tagaki 2006). Formerly, national education systems tended to emphasize the education of indigenous people to adapt to the local society and culture. However, the blurring of boundaries between societies and cultures due to increasing mobility of people across national boundaries and the interconnectedness and interdependence of global economies have given a new impetus to universities to internationalize their curriculum. Approaches to internationalizing the higher education curriculum include, among others:

- study abroad programmes at foreign partner institutions incorporating credit transfers into the home credit system and in some cases in the development of double or joint degree awards separately or together with partner institutions (Huang 2007);
- language and culture programmes;
- incorporating an international dimension in existing programmes through adding comparative elements, case studies of other national contexts, work and learning experience in another country;
- cross-cultural communication and understanding programmes.

A major impediment to internationalizing university curriculum is that most of the developments are piecemeal and do not have a campus-wide focus. Research shows that developments in this area are often not embedded in an institutional-based culture but in a small sample of keen and interested individuals in some departments (Boegh and Tagaki 2006). Since such changes often have implications on developments across the universities, internationalizing the university curriculum needs to be viewed as a campus-wide rather than individual subject initiative.

Collaborative international research

Supported by a network of seven research councils, UK higher education institutions are strongly encouraged to forge collaborative ventures with the best researchers from around the world and to promote the movement of researchers to and from the UK. The research councils in return offer access to databases, facilities, and resources to enable researchers to influence the international research agenda and to promote the UK as a world centre for research and innovation (Research Councils UK 2007). The Research Assessment Exercise (RAE), the key mechanism through which research activity and quality are assessed in UK universities as a precursor to institutional funding decisions, places a premium on research with an international impact. Thus, academics in UK higher education are strongly encouraged to engage with research problems and partners at an international level. In addition, the government, through the Prime Minister's Higher Education Initiative, sponsors research and development projects with international partners in Africa, South Africa and India (DfES 2006). Academics tend to access funding for these projects on a competitive basis. This is part of the government's long-term vision to secure the position of the UK as a global leader in international education.

Borderless and cross-border higher education

As indicated earlier, borderless higher education is premised on the affordances brought about by developments in ICT. Notable educational innovations deriving from advances in ICT include **e-learning** and **m-learning** (mobile learning). It is now possible to have synchronous lectures with overseas partners albeit within the constraints of continental world time differences. Thus, e-learning is naturally suited to distance learning and flexible learning, but can also be used in conjunction with face-to-face teaching, in which case the term 'blended learning' is commonly used.

In higher education especially, the increasing tendency is to create virtual learning environment (VLEs), which are sometimes combined with a Management Information System (MIS) to create a managed learning system, in which all aspects of a course are handled through a consistent user interface standard throughout the institution. A growing number of physical universities, as well as newer online-only colleges, have begun to offer degree and certificate programmes via the Internet at a wide range of levels and in a wide range of disciplines. While some programmes require students to attend campus classes or orientations, many are delivered completely online. In addition, several universities offer online student support services, such as online advising and registration, e-counselling, online textbook purchase, student governments and student newspapers. e-learning can also refer to educational web sites such as those offering learning scenarios, worksheets and interactive exercises for children. The term is also used extensively in the business sector where it generally refers to cost-effective online training. Key advantages of e-learning are flexibility, convenience and the ability to work at any place where an Internet connection is available and at one's own pace.

e-classes are asynchronous which allows learners to participate and complete coursework around their daily commitments. This makes an e-learning education a viable option for those who have family or work responsibilities or cannot participate easily due to disability. There are also transportation cost (and time) benefits in not having to commute to and from campus. Other advantages of e-learning are the ability to communicate with fellow classmates independent of metrical distance, a greater adaptability to learners' needs, more variety in learning experience with the use of multimedia and the non-verbal presentation of teaching material. Streamed video recorded lectures and MP3 files provide visual and audio learning that can be reviewed as often as needed. For organizations with distributed and constantly changing learners (for example, restaurant staff), e-learning has considerable benefits when compared with organizing classroom training. Lack of face-to-face experience, lag time in receiving feedback and learning isolation have often been cited as the major drawbacks to e-learning.

Involvement and investment in e-learning and m-learning technologies have thus become strategies of choice for institutions seeking to raise their international profile.

Marketing institutional internationalization: emerging models

Internationalization of the university is a fairly recent phenomenon. Marketing support of institutional internationalization activities takes a number of forms, some of which are more developed than others. Three of the most prominent ones are discussed below.

Marketing internationalization through the university mission

A review of the strategic mission and vision statements of 37 universities in the UK (Maringe 2007) revealed the following interesting findings:

- The word 'international' is used as a benchmark for indicating the high standards to which universities aspire to associate.
- 'International' is used more frequently than other terms closely associated with it such as global, trans-national or regional.
- With the exception of a few institutions, the key purpose of universities as summarized in the purpose statements is that of creating internationally recognized research, scholarship and learning.

- The ultimate vision of the majority of universities is to become recognized internationally as world class in their key endeavours of research, teaching and service.
- Specific university aims encapsulate a desire to produce research of international excellence; provide internationally distinctive learning experiences; expose staff and students to stimulating international environments; and promote the international reputation of the institution.
- A key area of sustained activity for many universities is to promote the recruitment of international students.

It could thus be said that becoming international is a key priority of higher education and that many institutions use their publicly available mission and vision statements to disseminate this key strategic intent.

University brand marketing

Many universities, like their business counterparts, use brand logos to represent the core values and portray their corporate images to the rest of the world. The logos provide a visual university identity which plays a crucial role in reinforcing core values and aspirations of the institution. Both the visual images and the words on the logo are carefully and painstakingly selected to define in the most accurate way what the university is about. The older universities tend to use images of old buildings and scripted crests written in some dead language, encapsulating the deep-seated values that drive the university. The images of old buildings help to connect the institution with the timeless age-old traditions that have helped make the institution what it is and for which it is most valued and cherished by those who have passed through it.

Images, however, are not always timeless. For example, the University of Southampton has used the dolphin as its visual identity, based on its well-established friendly and intelligent nature. Recent evidence, however, suggests that the dolphin has been overrated in terms of intelligence. On the back of this evidence, the university is actively reviewing its entire brand and is currently poised to break with traditions of more than a century.

Setting up offices and hot desks in overseas centres

There has been a trend towards the establishment of offshore offices in key markets, especially in Malaysia, India and China, where more than 25 universities have or have had offices. Offices are usually set up in the countries' capital cities and are generally run by locally recruited staff who have had past relationship with the UK. Although initial set-up investment is high, the anticipated benefits are high and quite significant. They include:

- reinforcement of the institutional brand through commitment to a specific country;
- offers of economies of travel costs for prospective students;
- offices to provide local support for walk-in enquiries, staff academic visits and local exhibitions;
- closer working with visa staff in the consulate or embassy on behalf of students;
- easier communication with local institutional contacts who can assist in the development of collaborations and partnerships.

Hot desk offices are a cheaper alternative and can be moved more easily to the ideal location when the need arises. Other universities have experimented with the idea of a roving country manager who visits countries at different times over the year. However, this approach offers little continuity and is often considered less satisfactory than the more permanent office-based infrastructure.

Overseas campuses and joint ventures

The spread of overseas campuses is increasing rapidly. The USA, Ireland and the UK have been identified as the most active players in this dimension of the internationalization of higher education. In the UK, the universities of Nottingham, Oxford and Liverpool have perhaps the best-developed programmes of overseas educational partnership programme in China, Malaysia and India. Key advantages associated with this development include:

- providing a ready environment for staff and students to learn cooperatively;
- providing a ready environment for staff to gain international academic experience necessary for their career growth and promotion;
- enhancing the reputation of the university as a global player in key educational markets;
- enhancing inter-country relations and understanding.

However, issues of quality maintenance; export controls; protection of intellectual property; maintenance of brand image and quality; and issues of corporate and individual taxes have been identified as significantly troublesome for universities operating in this area. As Altbach and Knight (2006) have argued, although many universities have adequate internal mechanisms for monitoring and delivering quality higher education, capacity for cross-cultural external quality assurance remains depressingly inadequate.

Summary

Internationalization is not a new phenomenon in universities, but it has assumed a more prominent profile, if not a central role, in the overall strategic mission of universities across the world. Although universities differ in their understanding and thus approach to internationalization, the multiple perspectives have led us to define the concept in the following way. We see internationalization as the coming together of multiple institutional groups to influence the university to embed an international perspective in its traditional tripartite mission of teaching, research and service. We use the term 'embed' deliberately to distinguish it from 'incorporating' which other authors have used in similar definitions. For us, incorporating suggests that minimal activity-based internationalization processes and other piecemeal activities could pass as adequate internationalization. To embed requires a greater integration into the culture and ethos of the institution and for us, unless that level is achieved, internationalization will remain a heartless concept difficult to elevate to the status of a discipline of inquiry.

In our view, we concur with Altbach and Knight (2006) that internationalization will become the major focus for university development in the future. However, we see the following as potential threats to the internationalization efforts of universities now and in the future:

- *Global warming*: This could become both an opportunity and threat for the future viability of institutions. It could become the next rallying point for researchers around the world as they try to find global solutions to this potential planetary catastrophe. It could also physically decimate large tracts of the world placing limits on human movement thus limiting rather than extending cultural integration and exchange.
- *Global terrorism*: Despite forecasts which predict that there will be 15 million students studying abroad in 2025 (OECD 2003) from the current 3 million, following 9/11, there has been a noticeable decline in international student numbers in both Australia and the USA since 2004. If global terrorism increases, it is possible that this could depress the internationalization processes of universities.
- *Tuition fees*: Many countries charge higher tuition fees for international students. As economic differentials between North and South grow, it may become increasingly difficult for individuals to afford the higher fees. Countries such as Germany which do not charge fees for international students are experiencing a huge surge

in international student recruitment. There is evidence which shows that international students who are allowed to work for about two years after graduating bring significantly more to the economy than the fees they pay for their tuition over the three years (Vickers and Bekhradnia 2007).

- *Visa restrictions*: Many students from outside the EU face severe visa restrictions to travel to key study destinations in the region. Even when these students come over to study here, they are often unable to participate in student exchange programmes because of limitations imposed by their visa restrictions.
- *Widening access and internal capacity*: In many of the world's best study destinations, widening and increasing participation in higher education have become core policy frameworks. The net effect is that internal capacity has been increased. This could depress desire to look elsewhere and thus limit cross-border movement of students.
- *Wider use of English as a medium of instruction*: Many countries in the EU and the rest of world are increasingly adopting English as a medium of instruction in higher education. Study of English language has been one of the most important reasons why students travel to the UK for higher education study. With more universities providing tuition in the language locally, the pull factor is weakened.
- *The expansion of e-learning facilities*: Even though e-learning facilitates internationalization, it may develop to an extent where people may find it unnecessary to travel for their higher education experience.
- *Quality assurance*: Although individual institutions have adequate capacity for internal quality monitoring, there is evidence of multiple barriers in establishing and monitoring external quality outside the institutions.
- *Staff resistance to internationalization*: Academic staff do not share agreement on whether pedagogy is more important than content in the design of international programmes (Bell 2004). In addition, they also feel uncomfortable making significant changes to what they should teach in the international curriculum. Institutions need to consider ways of raising the level of acceptance and equipping staff with skills and knowledge about the international context to facilitate their teaching.

8 Fundraising

Higher education currently needs money. Its economics are perhaps no better today than when described in Adam Smith's *The Wealth of Nations* ([1776] 1993) as, in fact, higher education has always needed money. Across the world, costs in higher education continue to increase due to infrastructural costs, academic support, competitive pressure and, of course, the costs of academics. Technological costs for cutting-edge research continue to rise and student demands for prestigious environments and celebrity lecturers mean that, for most colleges, fee income is just not enough to build laboratories and concert halls, furnish libraries with computers, expensive databases and books. The responsibility for raising this money falls upon the vice-chancellors. They are the leaders of the universities and the onus is on them to oversee plans for funding development, articulate their case to the board of governors and then engage fully with the process. They are the leaders in building the reputation of their university in the sense of selling for mutual gain. Their leadership adds legitimacy and creditability to the campaign; it demonstrates passion and inspires other to perform; it sets the tone and creates the spirit of the campaign.

The tradition of philanthropic giving in higher education is well established in the USA and is now growing in the UK. Most universities in the USA and now some in the UK too have development offices dedicated to raising donations and grants from private and public sources. Plans are drawn up of need from departments and approaches to donors are devised. Appeals to alumni are constructed and an integrated marketing approach is created, usually around the selling skills of the vice-chancellor, president or other 'appealing' personality.

The 2004 Report of the Voluntary Giving Task Force suggested that in the UK there is a real opportunity to increase income to universities through charitable giving. Such fundraising is a legitimate activity and the report claims there is evidence that the UK population may donate to universities in the same way as in the USA. Of course, the scale is very different. According to the Sutton Trust (2006), giving has recently grown in the UK, underpinned by increased investment in university development activities. The results of these efforts are becoming apparent, with UK universities estimating that they raised £450 million in philanthropic funds in 2004–05. While progress in the UK is being made, significant fundraising activity remains the preserve of the academic 'philanthropic elite'; 13 UK universities raised more than £5 million in 2004–05. Only Oxford and Cambridge compare with American universities, raising £185 million in 2004–05, holding endowments totalling £6 billion and achieving alumni giving rates of 10 per cent. The remaining UK higher education institutions have a combined endowment of £1.9 billion, and on average raised £1.6 million each and have annual giving rates from alumni of approximately 1 per cent.

The UK Government's £7.5m scheme of matched funding, intended to build development capacity within the sector, has helped, but may be considered too limited to have a significant impact and hardly bears comparison with the USA. Compared with charitable contributions to colleges and universities there in 2006, the UK attempts are paltry. In the USA, donations grew by 9.4 per cent in 2006, reaching $28 billion, according to the annual survey results from the Council for Aid to Education (CAE). The increase was fuelled by contributions from alumni and other individuals. Support from foundations, corporations, and other organizations increased also, but that increase was smaller. Stanford University raised more money from private donors than any other university and together with Harvard raised over $500 million (Stanford University, $911.16 million, and Harvard University, $594.94 million).

Just over half of the $28 billion raised in 2006 came directly from individuals. Alumni giving – the traditional base of higher education giving – grew by an impressive 18.3 per cent in 2006, while individuals other than alumni increased their giving by 14 per cent. Historically, alumni and foundations contribute the largest portions of charitable support of higher education institutions. Following this pattern, alumni giving represented 30 per cent and foundation support represented 25.4 per cent of the dollars contributed in 2006. Foundation giving increased by 1.4 per cent, after increasing 12.9 per cent in 2005. It is worth noting the effect that one single grant for $296 million had on the foundation giving total in 2005. However, even if the value of that grant were removed from the 2005 foundation estimate, the 2006 increase would still have been an impressive 5.9 per cent. Also, the report found, 29.9 per cent of foundation giving is from family foundations, emphasizing the fact that individuals, whether contributing directly or through a foundation, are the backbone of voluntary support of higher education. Corporate giving represents a smaller share of giving to higher education institutions – 16.4 per cent in 2006, an increase of 4.5 per cent on 2005.

In the recent Council for Advancement in Education report – *2004–05 Survey of Gift Revenue and Costs* – the main conclusions are set out below:

- Larger universities – with correspondingly larger fundraising offices – raise greater amounts of money than other institutions.
- Fundraising at UK universities is cost effective. The average fundraising cost across all respondents is 28p in £1.

In the UK, the Ross Group's survey (2007) provides the first comparable figures from the UK sector on the percentage of former university students who donate to their university. It found that only nine universities reported giving rates of 3 per cent or more, and a sector average of 1 per cent. Oxford and Cambridge record giving rates of around 10 per cent. Importantly, very few UK universities ask their contactable alumni every year to make a donation. These figures contrast with much higher levels across the Atlantic. The giving rates for US state universities, for example, can be up to 30 per cent and are typically around 15 per cent, and most universities make a point of contacting their alumni annually. Meanwhile the Ivy League universities demonstrate levels of annual giving which place them among the most effective fundraising operations in the world. The latest statistics for Princeton reveal an alumni giving rate of 61 per cent, and Yale, Harvard and Stanford have recorded figures of 45, 44 and 39 per cent respectively. There is a cultural barrier to giving to higher education in the UK which is rooted in the notion of higher education as a merit right, not a privilege.

Unsurprisingly, the gap between endowment levels in the UK and the USA remains a gulf. As in 2002, the total value of the ten largest endowments held by American universities, at almost £54 billion, dwarfs that held by UK universities at just £6.9 billion. In fact, Harvard's endowment of £13.4 billion is £5.5 billion more than all the UK universities combined. Yale, Stanford, Texas and Princeton also have individual funds of over £5 billion – higher than any single UK university. Only two UK universities – Cambridge and Oxford – have endowments over £1 billion and would be placed seventh and eighth respectively in the US top ten.

How then can nations other than the USA lead such campaigns and how can they be conducted within the marketing and strategy model we have proposed? Is it, as the Voluntary Giving Task Force on developing increased funds suggests, merely because UK universities have not solicited donations with the professional and systematic manner habitual in the USA? We are not sure. Nor do we believe that high returns to investment in fundraising will be achieved equally by the whole higher education sector. However, UK government support in increasing matched funding of up to £200 million over three years, and its new scheme of providing an additional £7.5 million of matched funding, is certainly offering more than just rhetoric.

According to The Sutton Trust, an expanding cadre of development professionals across the sector is emerging, underpinned by the government's matched funding scheme, to develop capacity in this area. One concern expressed by some of the leading fundraisers in the sector is that the rapid expansion of development offices has outstripped the supply of suitably qualified development professionals. It is currently an employees' market, with salaries rising significantly and universities having to recruit from the USA and Canada. In some universities this has had the unfortunate effect of fuelling further scepticism of the value of fundraising among academics – many of whom are paid much less than senior development professionals.

Another concern in this fledgling market is that very few senior university figures (such as vice-chancellors, chancellors and principals) have been given the clear fundraising remit that was one of the key recommendations of the Task Force's report. It would be a considerable boost to a university's fundraising efforts if, for instance, its chancellor was paid to undertake development activity for two or three days each week. Not only would such a move generate more revenue, it would also help to underline the key role of development work in delivering the university's overall academic priorities. There is a paucity of development professionals at the most senior levels. We could only identify two fundraising appointments at the pro-vice-chancellor level – at Oxford and Edinburgh Universities – in the sector. The current generation of vice-chancellors is generally well aware of fundraising opportunities, but more senior level appointments are needed to inculcate the cultural change needed at the very top level of university administration. Only then is it likely that fundraising will emerge as a centrally accepted activity in academic life in the UK.

In this chapter we will attempt an analysis of actions advocated by successful American fundraisers and then contextualize them in the marketing strategy and implementation model we have developed. We agree with the Task Force on the two key principles of voluntary giving. First, the role of voluntary giving should be to support the development of the university towards achieving excellence, not maintenance or core funding. It is not a substitute for other sources of higher education funding, particularly public funding. Second, universities have a responsibility to encourage commitment of stakeholders to their future success and to solicit donations from those that can afford it. Higher education universities invariably have a charitable role and should, in turn, take full advantage of this in asking for financial support.

To start with, universities need to develop a stance on receiving gifts, whether they are annual alumni gifts, endowments or capital gifts in forms such as cash, pledges, securities, property or gifts in kind. There is a wide range of guides and resources available, as one would expect, mainly from the USA. They cover such issues as campaign models, making a case for support, recruiting, educating, motivating and defining roles for volunteers, building an annual fund, cultivation and solicitation of major gifts, approaching corporate donors and concluding a campaign. A review of all these topics is beyond the scope of this chapter. What we can address are three specific aspects:

- choosing a campaign model and a case for support;
- donor motivation;
- realizing the gifts.

Gottfried and Johnson (2005) undertook an interesting study into the drivers of gifting and the relationship of gifts and solicitation. Past literature in the field of giving in higher education has found that donations depend on particular college characteristics such as total number of students, and therefore future graduates, as well as many others. Baade and Sundberg (1996), for instance, found that these factors include the income of students' parents, the effort that universities make to solicit donations and the quality of their league tables. In addition to university-specific characteristics, success in athletics has been shown to affect donations. Coughlin and Erekson (1985), in a cross-sectional study, reveal that attendance, post-season play and overall season winning percentage all have been shown to have a positive effect on donations to the schools' athletic programmes. The effects of athletic success on non-athletic university donations are less convincing; athletic success has no effect on non-alumni donations and a somewhat positive effect on alumni donations.

Leslie and Ramey (1988) demonstrate that US colleges' efforts in soliciting donations have been shown to have a 'reactive' effect, meaning that increased donation solicitation may actually lead to lower levels of donations, although this result was not statistically significant. In Gottfried and Johnson's own study, with regard to their control variables the variable endowment is statistically significant at the 1 per cent level. They claim that their result refutes Oster (2001), who found that endowment had a negative 'crowding out' effect. We suspect that her result was limited by the fact that the sample size was significantly smaller and that the time period did not include major macroeconomic events that the former does consider.

Second, enrolment confirms our initial hypothesis that an increase in student body will yield an increase in the total sum donated. Third, football is predominantly statistically insignificant and negative in sign. This contrasts to previous literature in the field (Coughlin and Erekson 1985; Grimes and Chressanthis 1994; Baade and Sundberg 1996; Rhoads and Gerking 2000), which has historically demonstrated a positive relationship between football wins and alumni giving. In these, the authors examined a more extensive history of football wins and observed a positive effect of football on alumni giving. Fourth, ranking is significant and positive in the econometric regressions. There are two likely explanations: alumni reward a school for landing itself in the top tiered ranking, and the rankings provide additional visibility for those schools recognized. Although there are not many recent studies replicating these findings, until there is evidence to the contrary, we believe that these factors continue to exert an influence on alumni-sustained contribution to their *alma mater*.

As in all marketing activities, the premise upon which a campaign is built is a feasible proposition that is appealing, morally sound and representative of the ethos of the initiating university. It is at this very first step that the link with our notion of pro-educating is forged and we will clarify this in the final section of the chapter.

Choosing a campaign model and building a case for support

The campaign model is chosen to deliver the overall fundraising strategy. It is intentional solicitation from those who might share an interest with the university in developing its resources and satisfies the intrinsic and/or extrinsic needs of the donor. As Dove describes, a campaign 'delineates publicly a set of priorities to be met and dollars to be raised in a specific period of time' (2001: 25–6).

There are several campaign models in circulation. There are traditionally four: annual, capital, comprehensive and single-purpose. They differ in that the annual model (somewhat overtaken by relationship management) seeks to match income and expenditure by increasing funding in that year. Its value is for small-scale research activities or centres, but unlikely to be the core of any major institutional strategy. Capital campaigns are related to a specific and high value campaign designed to generate resources for capital expenditure. This expenditure helps the university to retain its lead or reposition itself, and to involve highly motivated professional and volunteer fundraisers in focusing attempts to raise money from existing and new donors. The third form of campaign is the comprehensive campaign, which integrates elements of annual, endowment and capital gifts. This is the most common approach, for it links new and established donors rather than neglecting the latter and builds a spirit of empathy and loyalty with the university. The final campaign model, the single-purpose, appeals to a specific segment of the donor community. It identifies a project to be funded – library, laboratory or business school – to those whose motivation is likely to be most engaged and then directs the campaign towards them.

These distinct campaigns focus on the donor as the subject, albeit a potentially different subject for each call for funds. Following the shift in emphasis in the marketing literature to relationship marketing, far more sophisticated marketing campaign models built on lifetime giving can be constructed. In these, the relationship between the alumni or corporate donor is followed, enhanced and nurtured so that the interests and the gifting potential of the donor are recognized and rewarded for increasing commitment to the university through increased gifting. As Table 8.1 shows, as the wealth of the individual grows, so does the potential for increased gifts.

Table 8.1 Individual wealth and size of gift

Form and increasing size of gift	Life stage (indicative age)
Annual gift	30
Upgraded annual gift	40
Special gift	50
Major gift	60
Capital gift	70
Estate gift	80

Source: Adapted from Dove (2001).

Understanding the alumni for whom the model works best is critical to the success of this type of campaign, but it requires detailed segmentation of the alumni base. Thiede (1998) offers a mechanism for organizing such a programme. This five-part programme requires:

- gathering information on current and prospective donors;
- identifying donor segments;
- fostering lifelong donor relationships through consistent, targeted communications;
- tracking performance through systematic analysis;
- ongoing evaluation and approval of donor performance.

This may or may not translate into other cultures but, in the USA at Indiana University Foundation, a simple segmentation model of age – under 45, 45–65 and over 65 – married or single, and over or under $75,000 annual income, created a segmentation matrix which reveals effective targeted campaigns when applied to benefactors.

Building and promoting a case for support

The case for support is the key document to a successful campaign. It explains the proposed plan for raising money; what it will be used on and, most importantly, who will lead the campaign. This document has to be clear and draw links between what the university is and what it will be, and how the planned campaign will enable this to happen. It needs to state the philosophy and values of the university and of those involved in the university as supporters of the campaign, most specifically its senior members. It should contain a summary of the university's social and academic accomplishments, statements about its new future and how the money will enable that vision to be made reality. After providing this background, the document needs to discuss the immediate and long-term development objectives and the plans for action on behalf of the donor to achieve this.

This document gives confidence to donors provided it is well argued, supported by those with integrity and speaks to them, bringing them into the community of common identity with the university. This of course is easier, as we have seen above, when that community carries endorsements of success from its local, national and international community. It thus links straight back to the nature of the university and what it really stands for. If its mission is indistinct and its culture not one of meritocracy, it has little to offer donors. Why should they identify with a university that gives them no added value? Raising funds is like the development of the overall marketing strategy we have explored in previous chapters. If it is based on deception it will not prompt the support of the alumni it has let down, nor the community that is its host. It must give the students more than the cost of education if it is to share the benefits of their subsequent success.

Donor motivation

Donor motivations for all causes have much in common and indeed are in competition. Greenfield (2002) suggests 11 reasons why people give to non-profit organizations:

- a desire to act charitably;
- ego satisfaction;
- public acclaim for philanthropists;
- religious directives;
- the worthy cause;
- the commonality of humanity;
- organizational public image;
- trust in the use of their money;
- good leadership in the recipient organization;
- the organization is financially sound;
- they were asked!

Donors achieve personal value from giving which exceeds their tax deduction – although this can help!

Specifically in higher education institutions in the USA, mutual self-interest seems to be the central theme of alumni giving. Seeing your school reach new heights of academic excellence certainly reflects well on those who have previously attended the school. For large corporate and individual donors there is the issue of immortality, civic responsibility and self-aggrandisement that many find irritating. So why doesn't it happen in the UK?

According to the Voluntary Giving Task Force, donors are unwilling to give unless they are convinced that their donations will assist the university in reaching its idealistic ambitions. Furthermore, donors will not give if they believe their money is replacing state support, so it is essential that substantial public investment continues alongside charitable giving. Importantly, philanthropic giving does not support the core activities of the university. Almost invariably it adds value and increases excellence that is rooted in adequate public support. In a recent US study, donor motivation was found to be highest when donors believed that the university would be a good steward of the gift and would use it wisely. They were motivated by their gift-giving to sustain academic excellence and to preserve the core values of the university, manifested in belief in its mission. The university needs to inspire them with its stability of fiscal leadership. Moreover, donors had a sense of loyalty to the university derived from the intrinsic joy of giving and knowing that it would make a difference.

Realizing the gifts

As Table 8.1 shows, the most important type of gifting is the annual fund. The annual fund is the foundation of fundraising efforts. To be successful a campaign needs to be personal. It should talk rather than seem to be mass marketing. It must be empathetic. It is not about what the university needs so much as why the alumni want to give. It must be professional, for there will be numerous other calls on the donors' generosity. Given these principles, the development of an on-going relationship based on the past, but building up a lifelong association, needs careful planning. The use of direct marketing, telemarketing, Internet, face-to-face contact through affinity groups (sports teams, graduation years, academic discipline and selection of profession) and special events (dinners, dances, tournaments, sales and auctions) all need to be built into a campaign, costed and implemented.

All these engagements are expensive. Annual fundraising requires rigorous budgeting and effective monitoring. As in all planned expenditure, critical performance indicators need to be developed to evaluate the success of the programme. Furthermore, if the American experience is anything to go by, they need volunteers to supplement and, in some cases, lead aspects of the campaign.

Volunteers offer help and influence and are often donors themselves. The tasks volunteers may undertake include assistance in planning and making arrangements for activities, identifying potential donors, contacting media to bring new networks to the universities, acting as hosts at events and thanking donors. The volunteers' recruitment depends upon the task. For instance, there is a need for high profile candidates for capital campaign leadership, while administrative help delivering the annual campaign needs volunteers who can commit time and dedication as well as being team players. As advocates of the donor programme, volunteers are also the strongest endorsers of the gifting plan of the university. Their contribution is valuable and, of course, some are more valuable than others. Those who are visible, successful, have peers in the other financial leaders of other communities and are self-assured about asking for contributions are the volunteers a campaign leader needs. Volunteers' good will is not enough; they must be part of the planning process and committed to the goals as well as the process of the campaign.

Volunteers need support from the development staff. The extent of the support depends on the experience of the university and its current culture, style and history. For this to happen, university development staff can act as mentors and then as advisors to volunteers' projects. They need to be educated in the ways of fundraising and the programme's objects. Their main need is to be trained in the tasks they will be asked to perform.

Planned giving, or a pledge, is deferred gifting and can be a stable and long-term source of income. Its value is in allowing institutions to plan when revenue will arrive. Pledges come in many forms; in response to solicitation by direct mail, telephone or Internet campaigns asking for pledges in the future, and from payroll deductions and alumni fundraising club fees – with associated privileges. To develop such a plan, sufficient numbers of target donors must exist, for instance, over 60, and the university must have coherent, moral and legal ways of accepting these donations. Evidence in the USA (Dove 2001) suggests that the motivation for such gifting can be religious conviction (Notre Dame University), gratitude for the benefits of the education gained, the desire to be recognized and the desire to leave a legacy. There are also the direct financial benefits of tax relief to the donors themselves. In the USA, where there is a tradition of philanthropic giving from the general public as well as the very wealthy, the tax laws are both rewarding and simple. The principle for gifting is being encouraged in the UK but the tax aspects are still somewhat complex.

Implementing such a programme requires professional help from lawyers and accountants to keep records. A heightened relationship needs to be built to ensure that donors realize the potential benefit of their gifts during their lifetime. Put bluntly, one needs to ensure they do not change their mind, for they may leave more! The importance of maintaining this relationship means nurturing both commitment and coherence of approach from senior managers – indeed, all staff, whether academic, administrative or voluntary – in helping to solicit gifts.

Communication with current and prospective donors is therefore critical. Their value to the university, the value of their gift and the impact of their legacy must all be brought from the future to the present. In such communications the message should be that it is their gift that is important, not their death. It may take the form of brochures, newsletters (both general and targeted mailings) and seminars. Much of this information may also be sent to professional advisors informing them of the security and financial responsiveness of the university and of the tax advantages that exist for their clients. This approach is clearly best where the advisors are alumni or practise in the locality of the university.

Major gifts are a matter of 'hard work, imagination, and good taste', says Dove (2001: 183). The hard work is evident in the identification and tracking of major gift prospects and their cultivation. This is a labour-intensive, personal programme performed by leaders of volunteers, the director of development and the vice-chancellor. It is a long-term task and needs to have its momentum maintained. Prospects need to be prioritized and effort put into soliciting their financial involvement in the university based on personal knowledge of the individual, their organization and their values. Engagement with these prospects requires good planning, well-prepared proposals (statement of need, proposed action, financial data and donor benefits) and good timing and closing skills. The most common errors are either to fail to ask for a gift or to ask for one that is not large enough. Furthermore, having made the proposal flexible, the development team needs to adjust to the newly discovered needs of the prospect.

If the major donor is cooperative, then their corporate motivations are likely to relate to the enhancement of their reputation, recruitment and social responsibility. In delivering their social responsibility, they may donate to a programme on child care, children at risk, cancer research or any other socially desirable activity undertaken by the university on their behalf. Donations can be indirect cash, allocation of their shares, benefits in kind, encouraging and supporting volunteering programmes, their professional services and sponsorships. Other major donations can come from foundations which might be independent, such as the Lilly Foundation, or corporate, such as the Exxon Foundation. In the same way as organizations need to be researched, so do foundations and although they may have explicit application procedures to follow, it is as important to take as much care in constructing proposals as when approaching organizations directly.

In all fundraising, there are ethical issues and a risk, particularly in major funding, that the amount offered infringes the university's ethical standards for receiving donations and that the fundraising activities may themselves overstep the mark. Policies and ethical standards equally apply to soliciting donations, where no undue pressure should be brought to bear on potential donors. Attendance at a university does not require gratitude in terms of time and money, even if the university so desires. There is a danger that the rights of donors and potential donors are overridden in the enthusiasm to achieve a campaign goal. These rights include knowledge of the destination of their donation, how it will be used and accounted for, and whether their name will be used or not. Other issues arise from major donations where the donor makes demands. Interference with academic freedoms to publish freely, suppression of research findings and unwarranted interference in research agenda need to be resisted by the institutional internal policies. In the USA, there are professional guidelines issued by the Association of Fundraising Professionals and these offer advice not only on the form of solicitation that is appropriate, but also on the motivation behind the fundraising.

The campaign development and types of donors have only briefly been discussed here and there is a range of literature that can be consulted which offers insights, practical discussions and actual processes to develop a gifting plan. We have focused on gifting that is relevant to the goals of the university, not metamorphosing the university's values into a compelling commodity to be sold for the donor's self-gratification. Universities that believe in themselves, offer worthy educational experiences to their students and are well led tend, in the long run, to attract funding of a type that is appropriate for their values. The rejection by Nottingham University of money from a cigarette producer to fund cancer research is a case in point.

However, there is always a risk to the values and reputation of an institution in accepting donations and, indeed, in seeking them. The university development team is there to support the goals of the institution, not have their fundraising successes determine the nature of the institution they are seeking to help. Clear guidelines are essential on whose money is acceptable, which industries (sex, weapon, cigarettes or alcohol) or countries (apartheid South Africa) are taboo, and what conditions can be attached to gifts to prevent future problems and disharmonies in the university communities that are being supported.

Summary

In the context of our pro-educating model, a fundraising campaign needs to embody the temporality of giving to a university whose own temporal existence ought to transcend the present. This is difficult in the consumer-led immediacy of our current society, as gifts are for the unknown future, one when the giver believes can be shaped by the values of the institution in ways they find agreeable. This requires, as we have seen, fundraising leadership and adherence to a form of education that has worldly benefits. Donors need existentially to trust in the learning process provision of the university and in those who are currently involved in the learning process. Their money may provide a physical manifestation for the university, but its value is with bricks and mortar, the use to which the books and software are put, and the social contribution to be made by graduates to their way of being. This trust is at the core of the campaign plan. It shapes the approach to donors and it gives a reason to believe in the unknowable from which the legitimacy of the university is given and taken. Finally, if we market in a way that encourages learner self-trust, fundraising campaigns must convince donors that they should sacrifice their consumption, bought with their income, for the betterment of others in the future. This is a tall order and requires cultural change as well as persuasive argument. Besides that, donors must be convinced their sacrifice better serves their goals for a brighter future than by being donated to other good causes or communities to which they belong.

In the UK, the argument that a university degree gives greater economic pay-back is just a valid as it is in the USA. However, there the gifting ideology is more grounded as a substitute for welfare economics and because of this American generosity is great. If the only reason to give to a university was to enable another generation to become richer, as this might include their own children, a sense of self-interest would be apparent; gifting would be merely to satisfy the future enrolment of their children. This is not true of the USA, where the higher education system does mainly retain a strong liberal arts undergraduate ethos. The message that needs to be imparted to the UK is that education for the sake of money will not lead to donating; education for all our futures might.

9 Pricing what is valuable and worthy

The structure of higher education is changing. The old continental notion of higher education as a public good, paid for by the state and then exported to its colonies, has had its day almost everywhere. Today the private sector of higher education is responsible for about 25–30 per cent of total global enrolments and this figure continues to grow.

This change has been mostly to match growing demand, demand that governments cannot afford to satisfy and that private profit and non-profit institutions are much better placed to meet. These institutions, although supported indirectly by government (research projects, tuition fees and grants), need to pay for most of their expenditure through student fees. Furthermore, state systems themselves have to reconcile their desire for expanding participation with the need for students to pay enrolment fees. This is to satisfy the growing imperative to create a large number of graduates to fuel economic expansion. In turn, the market thus created affects academics, who naturally follow the salaries, the reduced teaching hours and the better facilities. It leaves all those involved in the market with the problem of money: how do they get enough to compete and survive? This chapter mainly discusses the pricing of student fees while recognizing the other sources of income available to the marketing team: consultancy, educational services, research exploitation. Moreover, it does so in the context of value marketing, hence all other income can be priced using the same principles.

The issue of fees might be an unappealing aspect of higher education to academics and students, but not to the universities' administrators, for without them nothing will happen. Fees, and how to price them, are the new challenge for UK higher education as well as for the majority of European countries and remains an issue of educational policy. In the UK, the strategic shift from reliance on the centralized pricing policies of government and the block grants for teaching and research to a greater reliance on private sources of income has been significant in different institutions. Income can be derived from the utilization of resources – housing, canteens, restaurants, from existential acts of philanthropy and from research bids. More recently, the commercialization of research activities in what has become known as the 'entrepreneurial university' has offered, although not always delivered, the promise of considerable riches. The pricing of the use of these assets has mostly been in line with market principles; moving the price first to cover expenses and in response to the competitive pressures within and outside the sector from those providing similar educational services. Indeed, halls of residence price differentially by the quality and extent of their provision. However, for most institutions it is fee income that provides most revenue and which drives the recruitment and the financial strategy of the institution. So the links between fees, recruitment and university proposals to recruit students are intertwined with marketing! And it is not easy marketing. In the UK, a survey by Push.co.uk in 2007 predicts that those who began courses in 2006 will owe nearly £17,500 by the time they graduate, up 24 per cent on 2006. This is set to increase and those who commence in 2007 will, they predict, owe up to £21,500 when they graduate.

The discussion of what form fees should take and how they might best be presented to students and their sponsors, who are mainly family but include companies, is an ongoing debate. In the UK, the notion that higher education is some kind of right which ought to be delivered free, at the point of consumption, has emotional as well as political appeal. However, this has to be measured against the ability of the government to fund educational participation of the quality they desire and to select the fairest method of collection. This means how to collect the fees during the student's course, after the student has graduated – and sometimes never. Given such a central economic relationship it is not surprising that pricing, certainly in the UK but also elsewhere, is fundamentally a political as well as an economic issue.

The economic argument is that, if institutions are operating within a market then, for reasons of efficiency, prices should be set. If something is scarce, its price will be higher, so the flat fees arrangement of the UK and other countries is thus both inefficient and inequitable. It is inefficient because institutions have different costs, offer different products and reasonably well-informed consumers choose between them, so competitive prices should encourage institutions to function more efficiently. It is unfair for the same reason. Why should the student applying to a university other than the best pay the same as someone whose *alma mater* will increase their social capital much more?

In the remainder of this chapter we will not develop the issue of governments' financing of higher education. We accept that it is in flux and always politically sensitive and we will assume that their decision is to move toward some form of variable fees related to market pricing and which apply to services that the university has to offer. Specifically we will discuss the notion of a pricing strategy for the institution.

The true price for anything

Whoever pays the asking price for anything? Most of us do, in fact, if we are uninformed and have no other advantages such as network know-how or ability. The real price is not that indicated in a brochure, but the price for which the university offers its educational experience, calculated after discounts, grants or bursaries. Both the ticket price (meaning the advertised price) and the discount price form the pricing strategy and contribute to the value marketing proposition.

Reductions in price can be in the form of warranties, discounts (for example, to applicants from a particular school – not yet used, we hope), loyalty bonuses – for instance, taking a second degree at the same institution, or value-added additions for the same price. We believe these price reductions in the education market ought to be based on merit, which usually determines the real price of education. By this we mean that the distinctions between entitlements for achievements are complex. The achievement of an outcome criterion may be achieved through consideration and preparation, through intuition or through luck, but once an outcome has been achieved, the entitlement is established and it should be given.

In this sense students have a right to a grade regardless of their effort and indeed merit it, since their specific behaviour has conformed to the rules that determine the entitlement. In making the decision on entitlement, we have no need to make reference to the particular qualities of the individual. If the students did achieve the grade by luck or by privileged circumstances, home life, raw intelligence or class, they are entitled to the grade – but do they deserve the grade as much as a student who worked hard, overcame disadvantages and extended themselves? This is a valid question even if the criteria are not well reasoned or explicit. For example, suppose that it is a requirement of the driving test to know the 12 times table. This is not well reasoned but illustrates a situation where someone who can demonstrate knowledge is entitled, while someone who cannot is not. This is the difficulty of merit linked exclusively to explicit criteria and standards. It pays no attention to the endeavour and personal growth, which may be considered central to a liberal notion of higher education.

Merit is thus based on standards or criteria and is a common way to distribute goods and praise and, according to Stewart (1999), appears to underpin the major issues in higher education. If we adopt this view, then the application of **desert** to educational thinking is (following Rawls), secondary, for it requires a relationship between a person, the context of their actions and the specified goal. In the example of the grade, its entitlement is decided by the institution which is empowered to establish the criteria.

When entitlements are applied, they may be considered in two senses: (1) a formal notion of entitlement such as merit; and (2) a morally-rich notion that requires a particular kind of content. If we draw this distinction, it would enable us to say that the person who knows their 12 times table is entitled to the licence if following (1), whereas she does not if following (2), since this is obviously an inappropriate criterion for driving ability.

To distinguish between the two types of entitlement we refer to the second as 'desert'. Our use of the term in this way is controversial, for some (Rawls, for instance) would deign it irrelevant to any fair distribution, yet it is plausible. 'Desert' is usually applied to a three-place relationship and is backward-looking. Our use explicitly follows McLeod (1999) who considers it as something that binds three types of thing: (1) a subject; (2) an outcome deserved by the subject; and (3) a basis in virtue.

The main difference in the way in which we use desert is where the criteria for entitlement are created on the basis of virtue. In merit, no such constraint is applied. This is clearly shown in the driving test example. Our argument is that in higher education the desert use of entitlement is more reliable, if education is to be anything more than mere provision of work-based skills and if we are to avoid the risk of exploitation that is inherent in judging on merit alone.

Initially, however, we look at the UK and the USA and examine whether the real price is apparent from the ticket price for some, or even the majority of students.

The UK experience

Pricing and access are clearly related and in the UK this link is identified by the Office for Fair Access (2008). All 124 higher education institutions have submitted access agreements, at which time they estimated approximately £350 million per year would be spent on bursaries and scholarships that would benefit low income or other under-represented groups. This figure represents around a quarter of institutions' estimated additional fee income. In 2006–07 a typical bursary for a student on full state support at a higher education institution is around £1,000. The range is from £300 to £3,000. Some 90 per cent of higher education institutions charging the full fee offer bursaries to students above the statutory level for students on full state support.

Institutions are required to use some of the money raised through tuition fees to provide bursaries or other financial support for students from under-represented groups, or to fund outreach activities to encourage more applications from under-represented groups. Access agreements provide the details of their bursary support and outreach work. It is for an institution to decide, dependent on its access needs and priorities, what proportion of additional fee income it assigns to these activities. We do not prescribe levels of income to be spent, but institutions whose records suggest they have further to go in attracting a wider range of applications will be expected to be more ambitious in their support.

There are three basic models for offering bursaries:

- *a fixed bursary* – for example, providing £1,000 for students on full state support and £500 for those on partial state support;
- *a sliding scale* – for example, providing a bursary between £50 and £2,000 depending on the amount of family income and linked to eligibility levels for state support;
- *a link to the level of state support* – as a 'match' or as a percentage – for example, providing a bursary equal to 50 per cent of state support. Some 9 per cent of higher education institutions provide a non-means tested bursary to all of their students – these bursaries range from £200 to £1,000. A further 5 per cent of higher education institutions are providing support above the state support thresholds, but with a defined limit.

The US experience

The average tuition and fees costs in the USA depend on the type of institution: two-year college, four-year public or four-year private. For 2006–07 the average published charges for undergraduates were $2,272 for the two-year, $5,836 for the four-year public and $22,218 for the four-year private. These 'ticket prices' varied considerably. In the public sector very few four-year colleges charged less than $3,000 and only 8 per cent charged over $9,000. In the private sector almost 20 per cent charged less than $15,000, but over 22 per cent charged over $30,000.

However, these prices are considerably higher than is actually paid by most students, particularly if they come from lower- or middle-income households. The College Board (2007) estimates that grants from all sources plus federal tax credits and deductions cover about 40 per cent of published tuition fees for private four-year colleges, therefore the average $5,700 in institutional grants received per student covers more than 50 per cent of that sum. In the public sector, grants cover about 53 per cent of tuition and fees but cost less overall than for the private colleges, as the cost of living is mostly comparable.

These prices and deductions indicate a diverse market with informed consumers making choices on the value equation which make sense and they can afford. The value equation states that value is perceived worth divided by price. This equation is critical to pricing, for it leads, as we will see in the next section, to a number of fees and pricing strategies.

Pricing strategies

The institutional approach to pricing is central to its overall mission and from that to its position in the market place. Pricing is central to the sustainability of any institution and universities are no different. If the function of pricing, to borrow from the marketing literature (Doyle and Stern 2006), is to enhance the value for those paying, it is an important concept to consider as part of our pro-educating mix. Pricing for exploitation, for profit or for short-term gain is not the approach we would advocate. Increasing value does, however, allow prices to be raised above cost and so create a surplus to be used to enrich the offering of the university. It can be spent to increase the cost base in terms of academic quality, to increase and renovate existing assets or to develop an outreach programme in the UK or overseas. Moreover, increased surpluses enable active social policies which may increase the role the university plays in the community and provide student bursaries.

As a precursor to developing a sound pricing strategy, the university needs data. The data need to include detailed understanding of specific costs of the organization. The cost of student per programme is essential for informed pricing strategies, as are data collected from competitive intelligence and market research. External competitive data are not difficult to obtain, but the true cost of the provision needs to be known before discussing how to position the university via its pricing mechanism.

Many universities already make decisions about overheads for calculating the price they want to charge for research purposes. This cost, which reflects the cost of physical resources utilized by the research project, is often frighteningly high when first revealed to academics. However, if carefully calculated, the actual relevant cost before any cross-subsidizing between schools, plus the academic salaries, produces a fairly accurate cost for providing the service. When apportioned between activities, this can lead to a fairly accurate estimate cost per hour of student tuition within a specific discipline. The breakeven cost will admittedly include a mix of fixed and variable costs, but this calculation is a good and quick indicator of the actual cost of providing the educational service outline as described in the course detail. There are important legal consequences of conforming to this document.

Having covered costs, the issue becomes one of value and how the mission of the university can best be revealed to students through pricing. While one could charge 'as much as the market will bear', this is merely adding on pricing as a measure of the other activities that the institution has achieved, rather than contributing to that positioning. Outside of education (and we hope they stay there), the nine main pricing strategies are illustrated in Table 9.1 which relates quality with price. It is predicated on the premise that if quality increases, then so can price. The real issue then is to understand what the relative quality is that they are providing, from the perspective of the consumers, the students and their family.

Table 9.1 The price – value matrix

	Low Price	Medium Price	High Price
High Value	Under-priced: value undercut by price	Attractive pricing: ideal for market penetration	Premium pricing: prestige, prominence
Medium Value	True bargain: may be temporary	Price and value are in balance, exclusive of other factors	Overpriced: informed buyers will eventually stay away but sales may be made to an unsophisticated market
Low Value	Cheap stuff	Turns sales into complaints	Risky to business and to sector

As the matrix shows, there is a basic understanding that in most instances you get what you pay for. A cheap, unaccredited Internet degree programme gives just that; a cheap and low quality product, experience and financial return (bottom left-hand corner), whereas the Harvard experience is clearly high quality and, for those paying full fees, the high cost gives a good return. For those paying less than full fees, the return becomes higher and the value equation more positive (top right-hand corner). Also implicit in this matrix are routes to changing position. Taking the positive direction first, high value courses in low-cost institutions can lead to a reputation that enhances the whole institution and the ability to raise price, for instance, work-based learning at Middlesex University. Of course, such a strategy is a long-term strategy, such as that adopted by some post-1992 universities, which is the opposite of the experience familiar to international students, where the price is in excess of the value obtainable in other countries (bottom right-hand corner). Of course most institutions are in the middle box. This is particularly true where there is government control of fees. This allows institutions which do not offer good value to hide behind the reputation of the section to which they belong. Fees set on value will change this and create real choice and diversity in the market.

Value for money

The value proposition

In the first place we need to determine the value of good higher education. In the UK, the current operational trend is metrics to assess declared levels of teaching assessments, and graduate employment or research performance. These two might be allowed to operate in the market to determine the value offered by institutions, but they do require clarity and understanding for them to be recognized by the consuming public. This is difficult, as in many cases, figures do not differentiate between graduates being employed or in further study. In general, figures show that at most institutions over 90 per cent of graduates were either employed or in further study after six months.

In the discourse of benefits, at least in the UK it is value as deferred income value that dominates. A recent report from Universities UK, the vice-chancellors' umbrella body, highlights the economic benefits associated with higher education qualification attainment in the UK. The report shows that gross additional lifetime earnings are now approximately £160,000 or between 20 and 25 per cent more for individuals with a higher education qualification than for those with two or more A-levels.

The main findings include:

- Financial benefit is greatest for men from lower socio-economic groups or from families from lower levels of income.
- The rate of return to the individual would be expected to rise from 12.1 per cent to 13.2 per cent following changes to the student finance package arising from the introduction of variable tuition fees.
- The benefits associated with higher education qualifications increase as graduates get older.
- Graduates are more likely to be employed compared to those with the next highest qualification and are more likely to return to employment following periods in unemployment or economic inactivity.
- Significant costs associated with higher education are borne by the state.

Higher education provides measurable returns for individuals globally well in excess of the potential rate of return on investing the money represented by the cost of undertaking a university course, according to an analysis by the OECD (2007). Taking into account both higher average earnings and lower risks of unemployment, university graduates stand to earn substantially more over their working lifetime than people who end their education at secondary level.

On the basis of an estimated private internal rate of return that takes account of these and other factors – including the time taken to earn a degree, tuition costs and taxes which have a negative impact on returns – an investment in higher education is clearly an attractive way for an individual to improve their prospects of building up wealth. In their 2000 report, *Education at a Glance*, the OECD spoke of the benefits of education where, on average across OECD countries, the proportion of 25–64-year-olds with a tertiary qualification and who are employed is eight percentage points higher than that for those who only have high school qualifications. This employment advantage is as high as 22 percentage points in Poland.

Education and earnings are closely linked, with education beyond high school bringing a particularly high premium. Earnings of university-level graduates in the 30–44 years age group are more than 80 per cent higher than the earnings of those who have completed only secondary education in the Czech Republic, Hungary, Portugal, the UK and the USA. In the USA, these earnings premiums are in fact 95 per cent for males and 91 per cent for females.

It is possible to contrast the benefits for individuals of attaining the next level of education in terms of higher average earnings, lower risk of unemployment and the public subsidies they receive during their studies with the costs that those individuals incur when studying, in terms of the tuition fees, lost earnings during their studies and higher tax rates later in life. The private returns for those obtaining a university degree or advanced research qualification immediately following earlier study are positive in all countries and particularly so for males in Hungary (19.8 per cent) and females in Finland (15.2 per cent). The returns for such students in the USA are 11.0 per cent for males and 7.9 per cent for females. For a 40-year-old returning to study, the rates of return are lower than those for students progressing immediately to the next level at an early age but still high in the USA at 7.4 per cent for males and 2.7 per cent for females.

Finally, a recent research project by Opinion Panel (2007) suggests students would accept a more market-oriented system and be prepared to pay more for what they perceive as quality and better job prospects. But the findings will alarm the universities already having to work hard to fill their places and facing the prospect of a downward spiral of charging less than competitors and having less money to spend on teaching staff and facilities. The average price that UK students would be prepared to pay is £4,800, according to the survey's 'price sensitivity meter'. Students were asked about fee levels they considered too expensive, expensive but tolerable, good value and too cheap to give good quality. There was little difference in attitudes between students of different social groups and postcodes.

Designing and delivering more customer value

Kotler (1998) argues that there are three ways to deliver more value to consumers than competitors. These are:

- Charge a lower price.
- Help the customer reduce their other costs.
- Add benefits that make the offer more attractive.

In each, the customer gets more value. Behind the value-pricing strategies there are a few important concepts:

- Customers are value conscious rather than price conscious, e.g. some customers will pay extra for prompt delivery.
- Customers assign a personal value to a product or service, e.g. a teenager is willing to pay a premium price for a concert performed by his idol.
- The selling price is based on the perceived value to customers rather than on the vendor's costs.

When customers evaluate competing products, they are usually comparing value. To increase the value of your products, you should either add benefits or reduce the perceived risk factors rather than resorting to reducing your price.

In UK higher education, the notion of lowest input cost has already been adopted by some universities. In the USA, where the marketing notion and differential pricing are perhaps most developed, the annual average costs (tuition and fees) are $2,272 to attend a two-year public college in 2006–07. This represents an increase of 4.1 per cent over the previous year. At $5,836, a public four-year college or university was up 6.3 per cent on the previous year. Finally, at $22,218, the private four-year colleges were up 5.9 per cent. This indicates it is not the only or even the main reason for the price difference. This is the problem with taking the lower cost option. The product is perceived as cheap and it is difficult to raise the pricing from that low level. Of course, in some service areas such as aviation and food stores, strategies of aggressive price reduction and cuts in the service level have been successful. Indeed, it is conceivable that on-line lectures in virtual campuses might manage savings in costs that can be passed on, but this is only possible if a commoditized notion of the degree is permitted to develop, where the degree is no more than a credential which signifies little. We seriously question if this approach is appropriate for higher education.

The second pricing method relates to helping customers reduce their costs. This can be achieved through local bussing, lower cost accommodation and food on site, lending or giving laptop computers to students or by endowments. In their early stage in the UK, these schemes in the USA provide full-time students with, according to the College Board (2007), on average about $9,000 of aid per year in the form of grants and tax benefits in private four-year institutions, $3,000 in public four-year institutions and $2,200 in public two-year colleges. Even given these discounts, inflation-adjusted fees have risen rapidly since 2001. Therefore this approach does have the potential to represent the institution as high cost and high value to many who attend. This seems a sensible pricing strategy for many institutions.

The third approach is to offer more benefits to the customer for the price they pay. In the UK marketplace, as we saw in the previously discussed research, the organization best able to capitalize on this position is the Russell Group whose reputation, if not their undergraduate teaching, offers high social capital when students leave the institution and enter the job market. Moreover, its reputation offers strong links with high quality, network international institutions for research. Further evidence in the UK is provided from the London School of Economics' Centre for the Economics of Education in a paper entitled *Does it Pay to Attend a Prestigious University?* The UK higher education system has to date been characterized by all undergraduate students paying the same price irrespective of the institution attended. Recently, a group of research-orientated universities has been arguing that the higher average earnings achieved by its graduates stems from the quality of the teaching provided. In various scenarios, they estimate a fee differential between prestigious and less prestigious universities of £2,950 to £7,250. This range of tuition fees is in line with the current inter-quartile range observed in the USA among private institutions which have greater freedom in setting their tuition fees.

All these positions are viable and encouraged by the UK government which is looking for a truly diverse higher education sector. Pricing is a significant sign of the position and the benefits exchanged for a high market price.

Presentation of price

A study published by Pure Potential, an independent campaign group which aims to increase access to university, shows that 75 per cent of bright Year 12 state school students feel they do not understand university tuition fees. This is 12 per cent more than last year. The survey shows that this year's school leavers are just as anxious and uninformed about the higher education choices available to them as pupils were 12 months ago. Most know little or nothing at all about the financial support available to them at university (93 per cent compared with 95 per cent in 2006) and 29 per cent are less likely to go to university because of tuition fees – a 2 per cent increase on last year's figures. Some 30 per cent do not feel at all confident about university fees, up slightly from 28 per cent last year.

The study surveyed more than 3,000 lower-sixth level students from state schools and further education colleges throughout the UK in May 2008. The results mirror those published by the Office for Fair Access (OFFA) in 2006 that indicated that finances are not seen as a priority for most students. The university, the specific department and the location of the institution are much higher on their lists. It is not that the pupils are unaware of the need to pay fees, with many knowing fairly well how much, but that they are much less aware what grants, loans, bursaries and scholarship are and where they might find more information. Perhaps covering their own ignorance, much of the negative reaction was blamed on the universities who, they claimed, glossed over finances because they are trying to sell themselves. The conclusion of the report was that in terms of attitudes to finance the key issues are:

- Locating information.
- That finance was not a decisive issue for prospective students when choosing where to study – they do, however, expect this information to be available.
- Pupil knowledge of financial support packages is patchy, and little consideration is given to day-to-day living expenses.
- Most financial information is gained from school-based events, such as seminars, talks from higher education institution representatives and activities carried out in class.
- Financial information is not frequently accessed online and, from discussions with first year students, it would seem that the more informal information sources – such as forums and blogs – are used the most.

The most useful source, though, would appear to be university open days, when prospective students can ask about finances face-to-face and gather unmediated information (OFFA 2007).

From the marketer's point of view, this appears a price-insensitive market able to bear much higher fees due to the perceived value of the benefits from the fees payment. However, ignorance of the marketplace prevents a real free market from emerging and shelters the least effective institutions from bearing the brunt of the consumers' disapproval.

A practical way of achieving greater awareness is through the universities' websites. An interesting report by the OFFA is the Good Practice Checklist for inclusion on their websites, providing financial information targeted at students, their parents and their teachers (Figure 9.1). The conclusions of the research identified a number of points for good practice including:

- Co-opting an higher education institution marketing or communications professional onto the team responsible for publishing financial information on the website.
- Prioritizing student finance on the homepage.
- Using commonly understood terms, or terms familiar to the target audience, such as 'Student Finance' and 'Prospective Students', rather than 'Costs' or 'Undergraduates'.
- Providing advice on budgeting and using case studies.

Summary

Pricing for value, profit or equality is an issue for each higher education institution. In the UK, it is yet to develop meaningfully, whereas in the USA the value of a higher education lies in the institution chosen, its ability to add value to the further income or life chances of the student. Such management of pricing to reflect the institutional position within the market is an important part of the higher education marketer's role within the institution. In both the UK and in the USA, external pressures influence the limits within which prices can be charged and increased. While bursaries and grants do much to reduce the actual cost, there is a philosophy of blind acceptance among students of the judgements that have been passed on their ability to pay, clearly based more on merit than enrolment.

Yet fees do have a tendency to rise above inflation and the best universities in both the UK and the USA still remain beyond reach of those who start life with the least privileges.

We are not arguing against fees or private higher education, but we think a target participation rate of 50 per cent and a tendency for 'the public good' to be usurped by industry's private interests demand a revised distribution of the costs. And nor do we argue for trickery and the assertion of power over students via grants and bursaries. Somewhat like Kant, we argue for a fair price which reflects the institutions' costs, offered to everyone at the same price. These costs need to be clearly evident and able to be rationalized. The decision to give grants ought not to belong to public institutions but to the government, and all institutions ought to be able to charge what they can fairly justify. This puts the consumer in a much stronger buying position. The reputation, the teaching and the research skills are accurately priced into the institutional fees which, when coupled with the enrolment criteria, determine their target student market. The same goes for research, consultancy and other educational services offered by the university or college. We believe that this mixed economy of transparent pricing based on value added principles, with the government doing the social engineering, is the most appropriate way forward for the pricing of higher education and HEFCE, for instance, have value for money guidelines.

- **If you don't currently involve them, co-opt an higher education institution marketing or communications professional onto the team which puts financial information on the website** – this is likely to be the best and most efficient way of adapting the approach to the presentation of information to the web.
- **Carry out a prioritization exercise on the homepage** – what are the five or six key themes which you want to highlight to site users? Student finance should be one of them, and its pages should be directly accessible from the homepage. If this can be achieved, this 'quick win' is likely to solve many of the other difficulties faced by prospective students when trying to access financial information online.
- **Have as short a route as possible** from the homepage to the financial information – no more than three click throughs. Anything more that this, and the user tends to either leave the site altogether or to turn to the search function, which in most cases is not highly developed.
- **Use commonly understood language** such as 'Student Finance' and 'Prospective Students' rather than 'Costs' or 'Undergraduates'. It is vital to understand that many Widening Participation prospective students will not have any family history of higher education and so are also unlikely to have a strong grasp of the sector's language.
- **Be clear and concise** – use succinct headings, sub-headings and key information in bold. Avoid page folds and unnecessary scrolling.
- **Be consistent** – links and menus should be presented in the same format and in the same position throughout the site.
- **Do not contribute to information overload** – avoid blocks of text and pdfs. Wherever possible, make use of 'Want to know more? Click here'.
- **Include a basic overview** covering 'key questions' that link to the more detailed answers. Remember the key questions which prospective students want to see answered:

  What'll it cost?

  How can I cover those costs?

  What statutory support can I get?

  When and how do I have to repay this?

  How can I get that support?

  What other support is available?

- **Use tables and summary boxes** rather than long sections of text.
- **Provide advice on budgeting** with examples of average/standard costs.
- **Use case studies** as students are confident that they can use these as a starting point. The process will also help you to segment and target your prospective student population.
- **Use budget calculators too**, though they need to be simple and semi-populated with some data beforehand.

Figure 9.1 The Good Practice Checklist
Source: (OFFA 2007).

10 Reputation management

All organizations have a reputation which develops over a period of time. That reputation may be good or bad but, whatever it is, it plays a significant role in determining the entire business environment of the organization. The aim of this chapter is to explore the concept of organizational reputation, identify the various meanings attached to it and examine the extent to which those meanings can be applied to the higher education environment. Drawing on empirical evidence from the literature the chapter hopes to provide a broad framework for developing a reputation management strategy which is central to the success of higher education institutions.

The rainbow concept of reputation

The Financial Times ran an article on reputation management in March 2006 in which it was suggested that 'you only know what it is worth when it lies in tatters'. The implication is that organizations tend to think of their reputation in times of crisis and pay less attention to it when things are going smoothly. The ideas of reputation and reputation management are **rainbow concepts** because of the multiple shades of meanings attached to them. However, there appears to be a convergence of thought about good reputation and its importance to organizations. Fill (2006), for example, found that a good organizational reputation has a positive impact on business-to-business relations. In the context of higher education institutions, the importance of institutional relations at local, regional, national and international levels cannot be overstated. Most people will stop to listen when a Harvard professor proffers a view to the public about an important issue of national or international concern in a way that is distinctly different from that if the same view were suggested by someone from a less 'reputable' institution. The importance attached to public information and knowledge is thus closely associated with the originator of the message. In short, a reputable organization or person is judged as an authentic source of knowledge and the views espoused by such originators are often highly respected and well considered. As a concept, reputation has multiple meanings and interpretations and only a few of these will be dealt with here. Key perspectives on reputation include: the public relations perspective, the marketing communications perspective, the crisis/risk management perspective, and the corporate branding perspective. These are briefly dealt with in turn.

The public relations (PR) perspective

There is a belief among many in the field of management that the idea of reputation management is a direct outgrowth of the predecessor concept of public relations. Organizational chief executives, however, continue to see PR as mission critical (Campbell et al. 2006). Nevertheless, PR has its own reputation problems. It has sometimes been associated with organizational totalitarian propaganda (Hutton 1999) and as a field of spin and image (Moloney 2000). Although a variety of definitions of PR have been suggested, most appear to feel that it comprises those efforts used by management to identify and close the gap between how the organization is seen by its key publics and how it would like to be seen (Hayward 1998). PR has multiple roles including defending an organization from attack by competitors, publicizing its successes, building a long-term image and nurturing relationships with potential and current customers. However, many organizations use PR for crisis management and as a tool for handling complaints. In so doing, they reinforce the reactive rather than the creative purpose of PR and along with this, the idea that PR is about fire fighting. Indeed, it is often in times of crisis that organizations mobilize press conferences, begin to run staff workshops, groom senior executives for press and TV interviews and provide a sustained communication onslaught with their multiple publics. But closing the gap between perception and reality cannot be achieved on the spur of the moment. It is a process that requires ongoing investment of resources and effort and involves a deliberate strategy to create and nurture a relationship between the organization and those who seek and use its services. Thus although many of the processes or tools of public relations can be utilized for managing organizational reputation, the intended purposes are quite different.

The marketing communications perspective

While PR is about narrowing the gap between public perception and organizational reality, communication is considered to be a key strategy for transmitting intended organizational messages in a way which engages the public and secures its interest in and loyalty to the organization. Marketing communication uses multiple tools such as advertising, sales promotion, personal selling, PR and direct marketing in various combinations and degrees of intensity. There is a growing recognition in organizations of its evolution from an interventionist paradigm, which focused on redress, to a new, proactive communications ethos which seeks to build relationships between the organization and its several publics. This new 'audience-centred focus' (Fill 2006: 32) is aimed not so much at ameliorating current difficulties and challenges as encouraging a dialogue with stakeholders to influence the image and reputation of the organization.

The concept of corporate communications came into use in the latter part of the 1980s and has been associated with the need to translate corporate identity into corporate image (Ind 1992). Essentially the identity of an organization addresses three fundamental questions: who are we?; what business are we in?; and what do want to be? (Albert and Whetten 1985). Identity thus reflects the internal organizational vision underpinning the overall mission of the business. On the other hand, corporate image is externally determined, being the values and impressions held by stakeholders about an organization's identity. Corporate communication frameworks are designed to translate this internal vision into a public consciousness which helps to create positive relations across the stakeholder boundaries. A higher education institution which is viewed unfavourably by prospective students will need not only a radical re-examination of its product offering, but also an equally radical communication strategy to transform the existing negative identity into a favourable new image. To that extent, marketing communication performs a role similar to PR, aiming at bridging the gap between current perception and intended reality. In that context, it has influenced our conceptualization of the idea of reputation management.

The crisis/risk management perspective

At the start of this chapter we mentioned that many organizations do not worry about their reputation until it is in tatters. Before the emergence of a competitive higher education environment, institutions existed in a highly protected environment in which reputation was not a key element of their strategic management. Today, crisis management has become a key strategic element of many organizations. The need to have a set of procedures ready when a crisis visits an organization has become part of the long-term strategy of many organizations, including education. For example, there is a growing list of legal cases involving higher education staff and students across the world. Increasingly, students are concerned about value for money in learning and frequently have much to say about the nature and quality of

instruction, resources and sometimes even assessment. Institutions need to have planned courses of action when such situations occur. There are a variety of ways to profile and analyse institutional crises. For example, Fill (2006) suggests that crises can be categorized as likely or unlikely to occur. Although revoking a university award may be a very unlikely event, some institutions have found it difficult to maintain the honorary status awarded to prominent people who are judged by the international community as unworthy on account of the way they lead their lives in current circumstances. Such universities have reported recently that there is no precedent to these revocations and hence no institutional experience in managing these damaging scenarios. Other ways of categorizing crises include whether they are internally or externally controllable, although not mutually exclusive. A whole campus could come under terrorist attack, for example; a rather unlikely crisis for many institutions, but one whose control is largely external.

Many institutions have established crisis teams which meet regularly to review crisis procedures and even to rehearse crisis situations much like fire drills, and to consider responses in situations that the institution may not have experienced before. Because crises by their nature are newsworthy, institutions need to have trained spokespeople who can deal with the media. The key elements of good crisis management include establishing good media relations, having external agencies in place, rehearsing hypothetical scenarios, dealing in truth and not evasion, and the need for an established crisis management team (Fill 2006). Maintaining an organization's reputation remains a key goal for institutions. Crisis management provides yet another useful perspective to build upon our understanding of reputation management.

The corporate branding perspective

The concept of branding is a recent development in higher education and is strongly associated with the notion of organizational reputation. Kotler (2005) has noted that the art of marketing is the art of brand building while Lawlor (2007) suggests that if an organization is not a brand, then it is simply a commodity and argues that most educational institutions are commodities in that they do not differentiate themselves sufficiently from the competition. They end up competing on price and making themselves vulnerable in the process. A recent attempt to brand German higher education (DAAD 2007) against the background of increasing global competition from the USA, other EU countries and especially the UK, noted that the German branding proposition had to focus on:

- quality of study programmes;

- good value for money and not cheap study programmes;
- reliability;
- personal success and individualism;
- modern, but not trendy.

A quick fix for attracting customers in retail and similar organizations is to compete on price. However, in higher education, a bargain price does not help to attract students on a global scale. On the contrary, cheaper programmes are often negatively associated with low quality (Little et al. 1997; Ivy 2002). Branding is thus more than adjusting attributes to influence decisions. It connotes the building of a lasting image about a product or service which consumers or customers will feel eternally proud to be associated with. Lawlor (2007: 3) suggests that:

> Institutions with strong brand identity carry a halo of positive assumptions that build trust and confidence in the institution and lead to positive outcomes … such as students choosing to attend the institution; a reporter seeking a professor to quote in a new story; a legislator meeting with a campus representative or an alumnus deciding to make a major donation.

In business, when you increase the net worth of a company, you add value and thus build equity. According to Blythe (2006: 89), branding is: 'the culmination of a range of activities across the whole marketing mix, leading to a brand image which conveys a whole set of messages to the consumer'. The key is that branding involves the full range of marketing elements and is not a simple manipulation of one or two for short-term benefit. Ideally, the brand should have a positive impact on the consumer in terms of their self-image, the quality associated with the product or service, the cost (not the price), anticipated performance and differentiation from competing brands. The brand thus acts as a focus point of contact between the institution's efforts to create it, on the one hand, and the anticipated consumer benefits, on the other.

Once the benefits to the consumer have been established, branding brings several well-documented benefits to the organization in reverse. It protects the organization from competitors, creating 'a barrier to entry' which allows the organization flexibility of pricing policy. In a recent study sponsored by the Higher Education Academy on the impact of the new fees regime on students' attitudes to higher education, Foskett et al. (2006) found that prospective applicants were not overly concerned about price and would not trade a relatively high priced course offered in a prestigious university for a similar but low priced course offered by a less prestigious university. In addition, branding is a strong differentiating device. However, consumers do need to see the difference between an existing brand and those from competitors. Why, for example, would someone choose an MBA in one institution and not in another? Establishing why and how an institution's product differs from that of its competitors creates a sound basis for distinguishing organizational brands. Brands are also functional devices in that they help convey an image of its quality and expected performance to consumers. More significantly, brands act as risk reducers. In higher education, key risks associated with pursuing study at that level include opportunity cost and employment potential. An Oxbridge degree, for example, guarantees reduced risks due to opportunities for highly paid employment in prestigious organizations upon completion of studies.

There are four broad types of assets that are usually associated with an institution's brand and these can be used as tools for analysis and evaluation of organizational brands.

The first is referred to as the *brand awareness asset*. This refers to the strength of a brand's presence in the minds of consumers, measured in a variety of ways including brand recognition exercises, top of mind recall and dominant recall techniques. One of the long-term influences of the colonial educational experience has been that of leaving the indigenous population with a mental complex which places the education quality of the colonial master above that which became locally available in the postcolonial period. In Zimbabwe, for example, Maringe and Carter (2007) discovered that many prospective applicants to UK higher education associated all its provision with the Oxbridge brand. Thus the Oxbridge brand has a strong mental presence in the minds, not only of local populations within the UK, but across the globe and especially in former colonial countries.

The second asset is the *perceived product or service quality*. In higher education, university and subject rankings provide a useful proxy for quality, despite their many shortcomings (Altbach 2004). For example, Altbach has argued that rankings give privilege to the already privileged and tend to stress performance in some subjects over others. However, despite their shortcomings, many institutions continue to use their standing to prove their quality. Studies of the impact of rankings on institutions show that a common selling point for universities is their position on *The Guardian's* Good University Guide or the Times Higher Education university rankings. Because of the lack of identity of many institutions, the labels pre- and post-1992 tend to ascribe certain qualities often understood by the public about the nature and quality of offerings within these institutions. However, as Lawlor (2007: 5) finds: 'Association by category may be somewhat effective in the short term, but ultimately, each institution needs its own identity to create differentiation in the minds of its audiences and therefore avoid being a commodity.'

The third element of brand identity is what is known as *brand loyalty*. In education, and indeed other product and service sectors, brand loyalty creates strong word-of-mouth marketing which helps to create a formidable recruitment base. Satisfied alumni will significantly influence how others perceive the institution. In some universities, leavers are required to provide a final testimonial indicating whether their original expectations have been met by their experience over the years. Some of the best testaments are then used as marketing tools in programme prospectuses. To help maintain loyalty, alumni are offered a variety of incentives including lifelong free subscriptions to the library and other university services, subsidized attendance at institution-led conferences and reduced fees for siblings' university education.

Brand association is the fourth asset of brand identity. A department or university may offer Rhodes scholarships, ESRC bursaries, Fullbright funding or similar eminent educational support, and may associate itself with key celebrity figures, as at St Andrews University in Scotland where Prince William studied. These associations can add value to the brand equity. Similarly, the value of symbols such as the Nike 'swoosh' and Coca-Cola bottles and labels provide a visible identity for organizations helping to build value and thus increase the brand equity. For example, the University of Southampton has used a dolphin as its institutional logo for a long time. The rationale behind this was that the dolphin is known worldwide as a clever, friendly and intelligent animal. Such values have become deeply ingrained into the psyche of students and staff and the hope is that wider society will associate the institution with similar values as well. However, recent scientific evidence from South Africa (Manger 2006) suggests that the dolphin is not as intelligent as previously thought. In fact, its intelligence has been estimated to be slightly better than that of a goldfish. This new finding may not yet have universal support, but what it effectively does is to cast doubts about the wisdom of using the dolphin as a symbol of the university. Because of the uncertainty surrounding this issue, the university may begin to be associated with similar uncertainty and this could devalue the brand equity in the long term.

Creating a strong brand identity is thus a key component through which the reputation of organizations can be managed. So what then is reputation management?

What is reputation management?

A number of studies in the field of educational choice and decision-making have shown that institutional reputation is one of the strongest influencers of people's decisions when it comes to study destinations and subject or course choices (see, for example, Foskett 1995; Ivy 2002; Maringe 2004). Reputation is thus a key aspect of organizational development which requires strategic approaches in building, maintaining, and developing it. Essentially reputation is: 'an individual's reflection of the historical and accumulated impacts of previous identity cues' (Fill 2006: 435).

The concept of reflection subsumes image. There are many authors who view image and reputation as interchangeable ideas (Ditcher 1985; Dutton et al. 1994; Alvesson 1998). We agree with those who see the concepts not as interchangeable, but as strongly related (see, for example, Fill 2006). We see corporate image as the view that different audiences have about an organization resulting from the cues presented by the organization. In short, corporate image is what stakeholders perceive the organization to be. Reputation, on the other hand, is a deeper set of enduring images which are more difficult to erase from the public consciousness and, unlike images, are not solely based on immediate representations. Thus, while images can be transient, reputation tends to be more embedded. For example, the University of Zimbabwe evolved from being an elite and segregatory institution with an almost all white student population in the colonial era to a democratic, mass-based, mixed race and open institution following political independence in 1980. This transition marked changes in the corporate image of the institution. However, the institution's reputation as a centre of academic excellence in the country, on the continent and across the globe has been an enduring theme in both historical epochs. There is something more enduring in the notion of corporate reputation that may be transient in the idea of corporate image.

Organizations want to be associated with a strong and positive reputation and this has become for many universities a fundamental strategic aspect. The University of Southampton, for example, captures this notion of corporate reputation thus:

> The University of Southampton has a strategic aim to be a highly-regarded international university with a strong global profile. To achieve this aim the University is committed to developing a strong international research and teaching culture.

'Brand University of Southampton' thus represents an international institution with a global outlook. Does the dolphin image help to transmit this identity and in what ways? Since the dolphin is the most enduring image of this university, does it need to be supported by a few words to capture the ideas of being international and global? Is 'global' a risky concept too, given the variety of challenges associated with it?

The public are faced with multiple choices in the marketplace and the chances of seeing similar institutional strategic visions on university websites are likely to be high. Customers often want to know what really distinguishes one institution from another and this is what the institution needs to understand, and to devise mechanisms for the public also to understand.

Developing and maintaining a strong and positive reputation is thus of strategic significance to the institution.

First, a brand distinguishes the institution from competitors in a very specific and unique way. Second, it provides a support platform in times of organizational turbulence. The likelihood of survival of a powerful brand from a damaged reputation is higher than that of a weak brand. 'Brand McDonald', for example, continues to flourish despite the numerous high profile complaints about irresponsible eating and obesity. Animal rights' activists have fought battles with Oxford University over animal experiments, yet these programmes continue unabated because Oxford is a global front runner in medical innovation and development. Third, it provides a measure of the corporate value and finally, especially in the commercial and retail sector, it has a net effect on the profitability of the organization (Greyser 1996).

In order to build this strong message about the institutional distinctiveness, Lawlor (2007) has recommended what he calls the FACTS method:

- Focus
- Ask
- Clarify
- Tell
- Show

Focus on quality and the customer. The organization survives solely for the purposes of serving its customers. Its vision and purpose should therefore first and foremost be focused outside, on its customers, highlighting how it will help them not only to solve their problems, but do so both efficiently and effectively. The university should not be seen just as another place to come and study, but as a place to have life-changing experiences. That emphasis is likely to hit the quality and customer focus button in a way which makes the institution and its offerings unique and distinctive. In addition, as management gurus have shown us, the only view of quality that counts is that of the customer (Gerson 1993). When internally determined criteria for quality do not match those of customers, a quality gap is created which destabilizes the very foundation upon which reputations are built.

Ask customers what they need and want. A key challenge many face, especially established universities, is that of transforming themselves from being inward-looking and expert-centred to being outward, responsive and customer-focused organizations. Staff in many universities find it very uncomfortable, if not distasteful, to think of their relationship with students as being founded on a customer basis. This is not without deep-seated reason. Students are not purchasing a commodity from the university in the same way a person shops for and buys a television from a retailer.

Indeed, the product students derive from the university can be both tangible and intangible and in many ways is the outcome of the students' effort as much as that of the teachers. In addition, students wear many hats while on campus. For example, when they seek to enrol with the institution and request all sorts of advice and guidance, they may be wearing the 'customer' hat; when they learn and receive tuition in campus classrooms and laboratories, they could be wearing their 'client' hats; and they wear their 'campus citizen' hats when they exercise their rights defending themselves against perceived injustices. Thus to plan for the entire student experience on the basis of the customer concept alone may completely disregard other important roles they play during their time on campus. However, regardless of the type of hat students may wear as customers, citizens or clients, planning for their experience across the range of these roles requires a good understanding of their needs and wants. This is not just about responding to their needs and wants; it is about anticipating these through a strategic needs identification and analysis process that underpins all curriculum, management and administrative planning and development within the institution. Reputation is what remains in the minds of these students after they have left the institution. The likelihood of this being positive is enhanced if the student experience – the entire corporate brand – is developed around the needs of those who are likely to want to utilize its services and products.

Clarify your image, identity and product benefits. Many university institutions suffer from an image and identity crisis resulting from a range of causes. Identities and images are 'volatile social constructions, that although seemingly objective, base their significance and existence largely on the interpretive capabilities and preferences of their audiences' (Christensen and Askegaard 2001: 2).

Organizational identity, as discussed earlier, goes much deeper than the visible symbols and cues used to represent the organization. It is, in fact, the sum total of the symbols and artefacts designed and managed in order to communicate the ideal perception of the organization to its public. A variety of marketing communications techniques and strategies can be deployed to communicate this desired identity. On the other hand, organizational image refers to the reception of these communication efforts by the public – the public perception of the organization (see Margulies 1977; Christensen and Askegaard 2001). Thus identity is internally developed and driven, while image is externally constructed and fed back to the organization.

Organizations can learn about their image by conducting external organizational analyses, the results of which can be used to evaluate, reconstruct and redevelop the corporate identity. A key obstacle in these processes is that many staff within university organizations are unable to say what their institution stands for. They do not know their identity (Roberts and Maringe 2005). The importance of having a clear understanding of an organization's identity is fundamental. Investing time and resources in developing this identity is a necessary first step and basis for developing a desirable corporate image and for managing the long-term reputation of the organization.

Customers will maintain an organizational loyalty and in the process develop an intrinsic capacity to recruit and self-recruit, provided the organization can demonstrate an ability to deliver the benefits customers want. For students, the key benefits of higher education tend to be the promise of employment, the life-enhancing nature of the higher education product and experience, the opportunity to learn in a multicultural environment in the increasingly international higher education context, and the promise of higher than normal lifetime earnings to those who achieve higher education qualifications. Universities that have a demonstrable reputation for delivering these promises tend to enjoy student and alumnus patronage.

Tell customers about your differences clearly, consistently and frequently. Why should a student who wants to study medicine choose to do it in a specific university and not any other? Why should a member of staff seeking a professorial chair apply to one university and not to any other? Customers want to know what distinguishes institutions from each other. A university with a clear sense of self-identity and a good understanding of the competitor environment is more likely to know how it differs from its rivals or collaborators in the marketplace. The message of difference, not similarity, is what customers want to hear and ultimately constitutes a strong basis upon which customers make decisions. Once this clarity about how the organization differs from its competitors is achieved, the next stage is to keep telling the public. This can be achieved through utilizing a variety of communication channels to maximize the diffusion of the message. The message can also become a permanent part of the official university symbols, artefacts, letterheads, corporate gifts and paraphernalia, compliments slips and answerphone recorded messages, among others.

Show added value. This can be achieved by designing appropriate and appealing symbols, developing catchy slogans and associations and communicating these frequently and consistently with the public. Such symbols and verbal cues help to give the organization a corporate personality which helps with the development and consolidation of its identity.

An analytic and process model for reputation management

The above review has enabled us to develop a model for analysing the processes of reputation management which universities could utilize in attempts to develop their corporate identities and images. The model we propose has three key elements representing an interlocking system of ideas and principles:

- the institutional context;
- the institutional reputation framework;
- the strategy and operational framework.

Institutional context

Examining the broad context of the institution provides a necessary starting point for developing an institutional reputation management strategy. Key elements of this context must include:

- the socio-political and educational context;
- the policy framework at regional, national and international levels;
- key competitor strengths and weaknesses;
- institutional strengths and weaknesses;
- institutional mission, vision, goals, aims and objectives;
- the intended institutional distinctiveness and institutional brand proposition.

Institutional reputation framework

It will be important to consider a broad framework for conceptualizing the institutional reputation management process. The variety of perspectives which have been used as lenses for examining the idea of reputation in this chapter should be utilized in combination as, used alone, none of them reveals a complete picture about reputation management. The framework will thus comprise the following key elements:

- brand and branding element;
- public relations element;
- crisis management element;
- marketing communications element.

Ideally, the reputation management team should comprise individuals with specific or overlapping expertise in the above areas and it will be important to identify clearly what aspects of each of these elements need to inform the overall strategy for reputation management.

Strategy and operational framework

Key elements of the operational framework should incorporate the following fundamental principles:

- teams drawn inclusively and with task orientation;
- focus on quality;
- focus on customers;
- developing institutional identity and distinctiveness;
- communicating frequently and consistently;
- demonstrating added value;
- ongoing evaluation.

Key obstacles to brand development and reputation management

Research has identified a range of aspects that make it difficult to build a successful brand which is the cornerstone for the organization's reputation (Aaker 1998). Some of these are external, while others could be internal to the organization.

External barriers

Temptation to compete on price

The higher education experience is a relatively price-insensitive commodity. In fact, the cheaper a higher education product is, the more closely it is associated with low quality and mediocrity. However, there is a wide variety of consumers showing an equally variable range of preferences for higher education products and experiences. In developing countries, for example, and in poorly performing economic environments, consumers tend to be very price conscious. Maringe (2004), for example, identified that pre-graduate trained teachers had a strong preference for distance education programmes offered by the Zimbabwe Open University as opposed to similar programmes offered in more conventional universities. Among the main reasons for this preference, a key consideration was the costs involved (see also Foskett and Helmsley-Brown 2001; Ivy 2002). However, given that price is an all-embracing concept involving direct costs, indirect costs and opportunity costs among others, it is very difficult to put a price tag on an educational product. Sooner or later, consumers read into any attempt to lower the costs of an educational programme as, at best, an act of deception and, at worst, an indication of low quality. Rather, one should aim to associate the organization with the Harrod's of this world. A low price market may be attractive in the short term, but competing on that basis tends to push institutions off the status ladders. Reputation is built on quality and not on price, and quality rarely comes cheap.

Despite the prohibitively high cost involved in undertaking a Harvard Business School MBA degree course, their lists are usually full for the next seven academic years. Foskett at al. (2006) found that, despite the newly introduced variable fees in UK higher education, prospective students were unlikely to choose universities based on the price charged. The annual Roper Organization survey on brand choice has shown that since 1986 the major reason for consumer brand choice has been their experience with a product. Price has never been the top reason (Lawlor 2007).

Lack of distinctiveness

The proliferation of competitors in the higher education sector means that providers have to show how different they are from the competition. Why should consumers prefer your product over others? In a case study of a university department seeking to develop its mission and distinctiveness, Maringe (2007) found that academics tend to exist in small pockets of distinctiveness or as individual experts within the department. Rarely do they see themselves as part of a broader picture of the department. This individuality compromises the group effort to become a unified entity on which the organizational mission can be founded and developed. Without a mission to spell distinctiveness for the department or organization it becomes extremely difficult to lay the foundations upon which the organizational reputation can be built and developed. Another reason is that, as shown in a number of studies (see, for example, Maringe 2006), many staff in university departments are blissfully ignorant of the key distinctiveness of their department or organization. As such, the very foundations upon which the reputation of the organization could be built remain shaky, at best, and non-existent, at worst. There are researchers who have suggested that successful departments are dependent not so much on a common espoused vision, but on the presence and impact of big hitters, movers and shakers within those departments who often have distinctly divergent research agendas and share little among themselves except a passion for success in that at which they are good. The problem with basing organizational success on this philosophy is that the reputation of the organization survives in the presence of the high profile individuals but vanishes as soon as they take their expertise elsewhere.

Fragmented markets

Related to the above is the issue of a fragmented higher education market-place. Essentially, there are two broad higher education recruitment markets: the home and the overseas market. However, within these broad markets are multiple micro markets to which higher education institutions provide services. For example, in the home market there are distinct market segments such as those responding to specific subject and discipline studies, and demographic markets distinguished by characteristics such as gender and age especially. Adult learners, for example, demonstrate distinctly different decision-making processes and tend to prefer providers who specialize in part-time and other flexible modes of delivery (Roberts and Maringe 2005). Other examples are the geo-demographic markets which are based on issues such as travel distance and the location of the provider. There is evidence that many prospective higher education applicants seek places in institutions which are within 100 km radius (Tonks and Farr 1995; Farr 2002; Read et al. 2005). In a recent study on the diversification of recruitment markets for the UK Postgraduate Certificate in Education (PGCE) training, Maringe (2007) made some startling revelations. First, failure to recruit to quota in subjects such as mathematics and science was not related to a shortage of applicants in the market, but to a widespread failure by those in universities to realize that the recruitment market is highly diversified. This makes the continued reliance on traditional markets such as recent graduates for universities both inadequate and obsolete. Second, training schools continue to use a 'one size fits all' approach to attracting and recruiting PGCE students to their departments. This approach is based on the needs of recently graduated students and makes little or no appeal to the variety of potential applicants in industry, in research centres, in part-time research positions in universities, and among large groups of retrenched employees in technical organizations which close down periodically for a whole range of reasons.

Thus the problem of fragmented markets in higher education is a two-pronged issue. First, the existence of multiple markets places institutions in the dilemma of whether to provide a specialized and focused product, or a product that appeals to the broad mass of potential higher education applicants, hence developing distinctiveness becomes a major challenge for those choosing to market more broadly. As we have seen earlier, without a recognizable institutional distinctiveness, it is extremely difficult to develop a recognizable reputation with which higher education consumers want to associate. The second problem is a current failure in many higher education institutions to utilize effectively market segmentation techniques and strategies as a basis for understanding markets and subsequently develop products and services taking those needs into account.

Internal barriers

Among numerous internal barriers existing at individual institutional levels, three are the most prevalent in the UK higher education sector:

- *Underdeveloped branding strategies*: Branding has been shown in this chapter as being at the heart of the reputation and reputation management process. However, within many academic departments, excluding those with a management and marketing remit, there is a serious shortage of expertise with the appropriate background and experience to undertake and manage the branding and re-branding processes (Gray 1991; Foskett 1995; Smith et al. 1995; Ivy 2002; Maringe 2004). Many departments and institutions rely on external expertise to undertake these specialized processes yet, in the absence of a critical mass of internal knowledge and understanding, the prospects of developing a home-grown marketing orientation in higher education remain elusive.
- *Organizational resistance to innovation*: The forces driving educational institutions towards managerial and business models of operation are huge and currently appear irreversible. This inevitability is, however, often met with another obstacle in the form of organizational resistance to change. In particular, university academics feel most threatened by the sweeping changes which they claim are eroding and corrupting the very core of higher education. They allege these changes come about through processes that commodify education and strangle its underlying value as a liberating influence, reducing it to an instrumental product purchased in the same way as bread from a supermarket. Such arguments are, perhaps, as extreme as they may be misdirected, but constitute the basis upon which higher education marketization has been resisted by the internal academe.
- For many, marketing is about presentation while education is about substance. Grudgingly, therefore, higher education institutions are adopting the marketing orientation. In the UK and other developed nations, central or institutional and departmental/faculty marketing offices are now a common feature. However, recent evidence shows that there remains a 'them and us' relationship between academics and those employed in marketing roles within universities. The integrated model in which marketing becomes embedded into the core business of academic departments does not have a substantial existence in many institutions (Maringe 2005a). Hence, concepts such as branding and reputation management continue to be frowned upon and are viewed with suspicion, if not contempt, by academics in university departments.

● *Pressure to become profitable*: The business model that has taken over higher education requires university departments to be seen as cost centres. They have to generate sufficient revenue, recruit profitably and become self-sustaining rather than remain as recipients and spenders of external funds. In the last few years we have witnessed closure of chemistry and physics departments in some universities largely because they had become financial liabilities to their host institutions. In addition, there is pressure on universities to recruit from overseas, especially outside the EU, in order to generate required financial resources. This has had the net effect of increasing overseas enrolment, sometimes at the expense of local recruitment. There is anecdotal evidence in some departments that upward of 95 per cent of postgraduate students are from overseas. HESA (2005–6) figures actually show that, on average, 65 per cent of all postgraduates in the UK are from overseas while about 80 per cent of all research students are from overseas. While this has increased and perhaps enhanced the international character of UK higher education, there is also anecdotal evidence from institutional surveys that sections of these international student bodies prefer to learn alongside UK home students than to learn among themselves. The reputation which UK higher education has enjoyed as a destination for a truly international educational experience is thus being brought to question through decisions driven by a desire to become profitable.

Summary

Institutional reputation is one of the main, if not the key influencer of consumer decisions in higher education. As a concept, it has multiple meanings arising from the varied contexts in which it has been derived. The PR perspective sees reputation and reputation management as a tool for maintaining peace and good relations with the outside world. As such, its role is largely that of responding to rather than anticipating problems and organizational challenges. Reputation management in this sense becomes an exercise in closing the gap between external perception and an intended internal reality. It thus assumes an instrumental rather than a strategic significance. The marketing communications perspective performs a role similar to that of PR in viewing the purpose of reputation management similarly as bridging the gap between external perceptions of the institutional identity and the intended internal identity. The crisis management perspective assumes that the university, like any other form of business or commercial enterprise, is a risk-taking activity.

Institutions are continuously faced with crises and need to adopt a strategic approach to crisis management. A key purpose of crisis management is to keep organizational reputation intact. Finally, the corporate branding perspective helps us to understand reputation and reputation management. Kotler (2005) has argued that the art of marketing is the art of branding. The key pillars of strong brands tend to be quality, value for money, reliability and guarantee of personal success and individualism. These are elements which are associated with highly reputable educational institutions and sectors. Creating a strong brand is thus a key component by which the reputation of organization can be managed. This management is based on four broad principles: (1) focusing on quality; (2) maintaining a keen customer focus; (3) continuously building and enhancing the organizational image; and (4) maintaining a consistent and persistent communication strategy aimed at informing and learning from the public.

Based on the above, an analytic and process model for managing reputation is proposed. The model has three key elements including: keeping close and understanding the institutional context; developing an institutional reputation framework which incorporates the key perspectives described in the first part of this chapter; and putting in place a series of operational arrangements for the implementation and evaluation of the organizational reputation. The chapter concluded by looking at external and internal barriers to reputation management.

Despite assertions to the contrary, issues of image and identity are becoming as important as the academic disciplines taught in university classrooms. Christensen and Cheney (1994) and Cheney and Christensen (1999) have argued that the quest for visibility and credibility in a cluttered and sometimes hostile environment has made the questions of identity, image and reputation salient issues for organizations. Consumers in higher education show a closer affinity to organizations they consider reputable. Managing this reputation no longer can be left to chance but needs to be incorporated into the strategic vision of the organization.

11   Enrolment management

Enrolment is a broad concept that lies at the heart of the marketing effort and orientation of the university. We have developed in previous chapters the notion that marketing is about delivering value to those with whom the university has established or intends to establish a relationship. Without students, universities serve a limited purpose to society. Students are the *raison d'être* of universities, the most important reason for their existence. The need for a strategic management approach to student enrolment is thus paramount to the very existence and mission of universities.

This chapter is centrally concerned with exploring the concept of enrolment management and uses an expanded definition encompassing four broad activities. These relate to seeking the students; retaining them; graduating them; and utilizing their power of 'word of mouth' marketing to influence future enrolment of new students. It thus adopts a student life cycle approach to developing an effective strategy to managing the enrolment function of the university.

Defining the concepts

A plethora of terms are often used interchangeably with student enrolment. Among these, recruitment and admission are the expressions most closely related to enrolment and enrolment management. Research on enrolment and enrolment management suggests that the view people tend to have about enrolment and the conceptualization of the role of enrolment management in the academy is often tinted by their understanding of the concepts of recruitment and admission. We adopt a definition of enrolment which seeks to shift the focus from dealing with numbers and money to one that emphasizes the provision of a quality experience to students which helps them achieve their fullest potential in the course of their entire life cycle. It conveys this to students before joining, during the course and after they leave the university. In this definition, we consider recruitment and admission as primarily dealing with bringing students to the campus and ensuring that they register on programmes which the institution offers. We thus see them as two elements in a four-stage strategy for delivering value to students in their life course. The key elements which make up an enrolment strategy aimed at delivering this value thus include:

- recruitment;
- admissions;
- retention and graduation;
- post-qualifying relations.

Before we examine these elements, it is important to deal with the broader issues of institutional competitiveness which, to a very large extent, determine the place of the institution or department in the recruitment market.

Departmental/institutional competitiveness

Many universities today operate in a recruitment market where prospective students have to be actively sought and sometimes even prepared for courses on offer before they enrol as full-time students. Few, apart from Oxford and Cambridge in the UK, and Harvard, Yale and Princeton in the USA, have the luxury of being oversubscribed by well-qualified students and can therefore direct the bulk of their recruitment budgets towards selecting the best candidates for their programmes. A key requirement for developing successful recruitment strategies is for the institution to have a full grasp of its position in the competitive environment. We shall use Porter's five forces analysis, particularly because of its relevance to university environments in which the importance of gaining a competitive advantage is paramount. Porter (1990, 1998) has argued that organizations which seek to gain a competitive advantage over others should be adept at controlling and manipulating five significant forces or threats in their environments: the degree of rivalry; the threat of entry; threat of substitutes; buyer power; and supplier power. We shall briefly define and review the nature of these forces within the higher education context.

Curran (2001) has provided a framework which allows us to examine Porter's model within the context of higher education. He suggests that, in higher education, Porter's model could be utilized as an analytic tool to evaluate the competitive advantage of university departments in four critical areas.

First is what he terms 'factor conditions', involving the research orientation and accumulated wealth of the institution. He argues that departments with a competitive advantage demonstrate an ability to provide those factors of research production that enable departments to compete. Such factors include, among others, location desirability, physical resources, human resources, knowledge resources, access to influential networks and financial capital. In economic terms, these are the factors of production. A strategy used by many universities, especially when approaching research assessment exercises, is the recruitment of 'star academics' to bolster their research profiles and therefore gain a competitive advantage in terms of attracting further funding for studentships, IT provision and the establishment and development of new research centres.

Second are the demand conditions. The customers of higher education are varied and include students, society, the public and private sector organizations, funding agencies and government. Demand can broadly be measured both quantitatively and qualitatively. In quantitative terms, we can model recruitment patterns using tools such as recruitment forecasting as an estimate of demand. Using complex statistical formulae, some higher education institutions have ten-year projections of their recruitment requirements and annual projections based on demographic, geo-demographic and psychographic characteristics of the customer bases in both the domestic and international markets. In qualitative terms, demand can be measured on the basis of perceptions held by different segments of the customers about the usefulness of the institutional offering and the nature of benefits they seek from the organization.

Third are factors related to institutional brand influence. The chances of finding a successful department in a successful university are high. Likewise are the chances of finding a failing department in a failing university. Rarely do you find a successful department in a failing university. Institutional brand strength or eminence, measured on the basis of the global competitiveness of the university, is the key element that contributes to the success of departments. Through brand association, departments performing averagely in globally eminent universities tend to gain a competitive advantage over similar departments in less globally competitive institutions.

Fourth are factors which relate to the strength of departmental rivalry measured on the basis of pressure to compete exerted by other departments within the university and outside the university. The pressure could be exerted in one of two main ways; through direct competition or through collaboration. Both tend to result in what Pinch et al. (2003) have described as knowledge communities that harbour all kinds of knowledge from gossip, comment on forthcoming funding opportunities, advice on how to create a viable research strategy and experience with a particular methodology or idea. Proximity and easy access to current wisdom are important factors in the development of institutional competitiveness.

Curran has argued that these four factors act in concert rather than independently to drive institutional or departmental competitiveness and that, as in Porter's diamond system, 'departments that get all four corners of the diamond to reinforce each other are likely to be innovative and therefore maximize and sustain their competitive advantage' (Curran 2001: 402).

Exploring institutional/departmental recruitment context

Once the elements which drive departmental or institutional competitiveness have been identified and determined, the next important aspect to explore is the broad environment in which the department exists. The SWOT analysis model is probably the most widely used framework for analysing institutional contextual circumstances. The model first identifies current Strengths and Weaknesses and leading on from there, Opportunities to be maximized and Threats to be minimized or avoided. It is a flexible tool which can be applied both to organizations and individuals and provides an objective analytical framework for decision-making and planning. More recently, however, the PESTLE model has been developed to enable people to consider broader external factors impinging upon an organization. The factors involved are Political, Economic, Social, Technological, Legal and Environmental which both influence and determine change and development within an organization. Some scholars have tried to bring the two models together to provide a hybrid analytical framework that enables both decision making and planning on the one hand and environmental scanning and forecasting on the other hand. In Table 11.1 we briefly illustrate how the PESTLE and SWOT frameworks could be used to analyse the broad context of recruitment in UK higher education in general. It has to be emphasized that this framework provides a merely generic and generalized analysis of the higher education environment and some key issues and factors which impinge upon debate and decisions in the area of student recruitment. However, even though the impact of these issues on specific institutions cannot be broadly determined, it is safe to suggest that they provide a platform and framework within which institutions could begin to develop strategic recruitment plans.

A brief discussion of the political context of recruitment will be given here to illustrate how the various elements potentially hit institutional recruitment decisions and plans. In terms of strengths, it could be considered that the UK government's target of achieving 50 per cent enrolment of its adult population in higher education provides an external drive and stimulus for institutions to achieve higher recruitment targets. However, the

Table 11.1 Broad contextual analysis for recruitment planning

Contextual elements	Strengths	Weaknesses	Opportunities	Threats
Political	Political will to increase/widen participation in higher education	Political opposition from opposition parties	Funding increases with increased recruitment	Is higher education suited to the needs of the majority?
Economic	Strong national economy and willingness to support widening participation	The strength of the £ against other EU currencies	The introduction of the new fees regimes for higher education	Impact on post-graduate recruitment market
Social	Overall, positive societal values and opinions towards expanding access and increasing participation	Vulnerable societal groups continue to have lowest rates of participation in higher education	School values strongly supportive of progression to higher education	Potential marginalization of the vocational aspects of the curriculum
Techno-logical	Higher education institutions generally well endowed technologically	Lack of home-grown expertise in the utilization of technology	Availability of business models in human resources management	Rapid technological advances
Legal	Office for Fair Access to ensure parity in access across social groups	Sanctions for breach of access agreements not effective	Greater financial support available for widening participation initiatives	Established institutions
Environ-mental	University expansion has generally been associated with city and local development	Increased carbon emissions in local areas	Locally available cheap labour reserves for local economy	Impact on housing and social services especially for small local authorities

uncertainties of the political climate, with the Conservatives seeming likely to take over from Labour in the next few years and their party continuing to prevaricate on policy issues, provide an environment which could negatively affect long-term recruitment planning by universities. However, the government's promise to increase funding to institutions that successfully implement Widening Participation programmes provides useful opportunities for achieving recruitment targets on the back of increased revenue. Conversely, the continued internal debates in higher education institutions about whether higher education is suited to the needs of the majority of people, as envisaged by government, could become a source of internal inertia in the recruitment process in general.

Developing an institutional enrolment strategy

We see enrolment as an overarching concept that encompasses recruitment, admissions, financial decisions and retention of the students that the institution most wants to serve. Developing an institutional enrolment strategy thus includes:

- analysis of factors that influence enrolment including what attracts students and what causes them to leave before graduation;
- development and establishment of a compatible student–institution match in recruiting and admission;
- development of strategies aimed at facilitating student transition into the university;
- development of strategies that help retain students through adequate advice, counselling and mentoring;
- development of a customer services approach which places students at the top of the institutional priorities;
- development and promotion of a responsive, sensitive and proactive culture in the management and services delivery system.

Clearly the overall goal of an enrolment management strategy is the recruitment and retention of satisfied alumni-to-be. The institution needs to have a clear idea of the pull and push factors related to attracting and retaining students on campus. This aspect entails setting up an enrolment research team which periodically examines the factors that attract students to the institution and those that lead to non-completion and even rejection by potential students. What is critically important is to note that these factors do not remain fixed over time. Indeed, a key factor of attraction could be a deterrent a few years down the line. For example, we found that in one institution a strong attractive force at the inception of the university was its narrowly focused curriculum in the field of science education. However, a few years later the university suffered from a lack of international appeal and diversity emanating from this narrow focus with many potential students viewing the institution as a glorified teachers' college for science teachers (Maringe 2004).

Matching institution and student values is the key to successful recruitment and retention in the higher education sector. On one hand, this requires the institution to periodically audit and understand its own values. Our experience is that many universities and departments consider this as, at best, time-consuming and, at worst, a time-wasting exercise. Undoubtedly, the identification of a shared value system is a difficult and time-consuming process, yet without a system of shared and commonly understood values, the institution or department has little to guide its vision and mission. Organizations that do not have a system of values can indeed behave much like loose cannons, firing with reckless abandon and taking no notice of their impact in the same way as a tornado destroys a previously calm village.

Despite this, all the universities with which we have undertaken research in both the developed and less developed world (Maringe and Foskett 2002) have provided evidence of institutional strategy documents. However, what also seemed clear in our research is that, despite the existence of these value statements in public documents in these universities, many academic staff did not know the values of their organizations, and did not recall being a part of the identification of those values. It can therefore be argued that the mere existence of a values statement in a strategic document does not automatically translate into a shared system of values within the institution. This is why it is important for institutions to periodically revisit their values and assess whether existing values need to be retained, given the changes and new circumstances surrounding higher education in general and the specific institution in particular.

On the other hand, it is vitally important to have a sense of the personal values of staff and students as key customer groups within the university. Staff and students could be asked periodically to complete web-based questionnaires which help the institution to identify the overall value flows within the organization. There are statistical modelling tools which can be used to measure the level of integration between institutional and staff and student values. Theory suggests that the closer the integration, the more purposeful and energetic the organization becomes in tackling its goals and attaining its outcomes.

The provision of adequate social and academic support is at the heart of student retention and progression. This requires properly trained and skilled personnel to handle the complex demands of an increasingly diverse student population on UK higher education campuses. Three broad strategies have been identified as underpinning the support that students need during the course of their studies. These include student advice, guidance and mentoring. Advice and guidance in many universities are offered at two levels. There is often a students' advice centre based in the student union. At the academic level, students receive support through a system of personal tutors and international students' advisers.

Mentoring, more frequently referred to as the student buddy system, is a more recent development in UK higher education and is designed to allocate new students to returnees who provide a personal advice and guidance role over a range of issues such as where and how to get books in the library, where to go for fun and games after lectures, and how to survive the first year of the course. In one university we have studied the buddy system is reported to have directly resulted in a four-fold increase in the retention rate within the first two years of its introduction (Bennett 2006). Essentially the system involves training selected groups of returning students to provide a range of support to new students and being rewarded in a variety of ways for doing so over the academic year. Rewards for student buddies, or 'ambassadors' as they are called in some institutions, are made in the form of refunds or subsidies for accommodation and subsidized access to other services within the university and its partners, among others.

A key aspect of the enrolment strategy aimed specifically at achieving the maximum customer satisfaction is the development of a customer service culture and plan for the institution. Basically, a customer services culture is one that is underpinned by an institution-wide belief in the supremacy of the customer. This should be reflected in the key messages and symbols of the institution and portrayed in the mission and vision of the organization. Students as customers should not only be considered important: they should be made to feel important. High customer satisfaction – the extent to which customer expectations are met or surpassed (Gerson 1993) – should be a key goal of the institution. Getting staff to adopt a customer orientation is not always easy, especially in the university sector. As illustrated earlier, there still exists a considerable resistance within the higher education fraternity to the use of what is perceived as retail business language in the context of 'the serious business of educating people'. However, institutions that have actively embraced a customer services culture have tended to incorporate the following key elements into their plans and services:

- *A total organizational commitment to customer service*: This commitment must begin at the top and must be spelt out clearly in the mission and vision statement of the institution.
- *A commitment to knowing your customers completely*: Systems for knowing customers before they come to us, when they are with us, before they leave us and after they have left the institution should be put in place. A fundamental principle in setting up these systems is that the process should be ongoing.

- *A clear statement of the standards of service quality performance*: Having identified on an ongoing basis the likes and dislikes of customers, it is important to set the standards that customers will expect in the service encounters. For example, potential applicants want to know how long they need to wait for a response from the university following an enquiry for a place to study; how much support they will have from tutors in developing their assignments; the criteria for assessment for the various pieces of work they will be producing; and what support there is in developing their personal statements, among other things.
- *On-going management*: Enrolment management involves both academic and administrative staff in various capacities and roles. It is vitally important for all who come in contact with customers to have the requisite skills and understanding of the needs, likes and dislikes of customers as the basis for providing superior service.
- *Working towards continuous improvement*: Customers become accustomed to quality service and may begin to take it for granted. Strategies have thus to be found and developed which seek continuous improvement in order to enhance service quality and exceed customer expectations.

Techniques for implementing superior service quality

Some techniques have been found to be useful in implementing superior service quality: 'the key to satisfied customers is having them perceive that you met or exceeded their expectations in a specific situation' (Gerson 1993: 28). Among the many strategies described in the literature, three appear to have direct relevance to the higher education service delivery system:

- *Adding value.* Service encounters should endeavour to give more than the customers ordinarily expect. An email or telephone call to a prospective student just to find out how they are getting on with their application goes a long way to instilling confidence in the applicant about the important decision they are just about to make.
- *Understanding where quality problems exist in the service delivery process.* This requires staff training and continuous monitoring and reflection on the part of those at the front line of service delivery, and swift action in areas of potential difficulties.
- *Involving the customers in the quality monitoring process.* This can be achieved through a variety of mechanisms such as regular feedback questionnaires, suggestion boxes for innovative ideas, clear complaints procedures, and through incorporating the students' voice

by inviting them to have representation on key policy and operational committees within the university.

A strategy which provides vital information to assist with policy and implementation in all these areas is segmentation, to which we shall briefly turn in the next few sections.

Segmentation research: the basis for informed decisions in enrolment management

Recruitment markets are not homogenous entities. They comprise individuals and groups who differ in many ways and who may have even conflicting needs and requirements. Segmentation is basically the process of splitting a broadly heterogeneous recruitment group into smaller and more manageable homogeneous groups, towards which we can develop more targeted marketing messages, services and communication. The overarching purpose of segmentation is to enhance the chances of providing a 'customized service' which contributes towards greater customer satisfaction and retention.

The literature identifies five broad bases for segmentation of the recruitment market (see Chapter 6). The application of segmentation models yields useful data for a variety of decision-making at marketing, planning, teaching, curriculum and even assessment levels of the experience of students in higher education. It enables planners to know the markets in a more realistic way and the data produced can be used as a valid base for developing and planning the total experience of the students, including the service and service quality.

Towards a strategic enrolment management plan

Investing time and effort in developing a strategic enrolment management plan should be a key goal for institutions seeking to be effective in the volatile recruitment market. Most institutions will differentiate between home and international student recruitment markets. Each requires a different set of considerations and strategies and yet together they contribute towards bringing, keeping and delivering value to students, the most vital customers in universities. The development of a strategic enrolment management plan is thus at the heart of this concerted effort.

Like all other planning activities, there will be myriad models at the disposal of institutions. A review of such models from a variety of institutions suggests that, at a minimum, strategic enrolment management plans should include:

- *An institution's definition of enrolment management*: This enables the scope and extent of enrolment to be determined, which in turn determine the nature of activities and services to be provided through this strategy.
- *Action teams and enrolment champions*: Committee structures cannot be prescribed as much depends on local politics and organization. However, a clearly defined system of action groups should be identified which should work under and report to an institutional/ departmental committee under the chairmanship of a very senior member of staff or head of the department or institution. Many successful institutions have recruitment, retention and service action (managing expectations) working groups that organize the working of their groups and report to the institutional committee. The recruitment group would focus on recruitment, admissions, financial aid, orientation and related areas. The retention group would focus on advising, counselling, academic support and co-curricular activities. The service action group might look after issues such as identifying and developing service initiatives, promoting the service culture, articulating the institutional mission internally and monitoring changing dynamics in the recruitment market.
- *An enrolment management plan*: The plan should identify, beyond the issues above, a SWOT and PESTLE analysis, the enrolment goals and objectives within a stipulated time frame, clear success criteria, the research agenda, strategies for admissions, marketing and recruitment in both the domestic and international markets, strategies for retention in terms of advising and support services and, above all, an assessment plan for measuring success.

A few ideas about the nature of enrolment research would be useful at this point. The American College Testing Programme Post Secondary Survey Series (ACTPS) has developed a wide range of instruments used by a majority of institutions for the research aspects of the enrolment management of their institutions. A review of the enrolment management plans of some universities and departments has revealed that the focus of research in the enrolment area is around four main aspects, and most of the instruments tend to be adaptations of the ACTPS (visit www.act.org for further details):

- *School-leaver learner needs*: This is often administered as a survey exploring the perceived educational and personal needs of young post-school learners.
- *Adult or mature learner needs*: This is also administered as a survey exploring the perceived educational needs of adults who have been away from school for periods of time.

- *Student opinion survey*: This explores enrolled students' satisfaction with programmes, services and aspects of their university experience.
- *Entering students' survey*: This provides a variety of demographic, background and educational information about entering students.
- *Withdrawing/non-returning student survey*: This helps determine why students leave university before completing a degree.
- *Survey of academic advising*: This is used to determine the experience of students and their levels of satisfaction with the advisory roles of the institution.
- *Survey of post-secondary plans*: Used largely as an enrolment forecasting tool, it gives an indication of students' course and programme preferences.

Summary

Enrolment management is an overarching process within university systems that is at the heart of the development of a customer orientation. It utilizes a student life cycle approach to ensure the delivery of value to customers at every stage of their experience. Students' needs and expectations are determined on an ongoing basis, beginning before they actually arrive and continuing until they leave the institution. The information is used to inform service quality decisions at critical points of the life cycle. The ultimate goal of enrolment management is to provide an experience to students that matches or exceeds their expectations, so that when they eventually leave the institution they can become part of the most effective network of word-of-mouth marketers for the university. Delivering customer satisfaction is at the heart of enrolment management. Its planning thus cannot be left to chance and requires a strategic approach which utilizes research as its fundamental basis for decision-making.

12 The role of marketing

When we began this book we attempted to reveal a new, more educationally-grounded approach to the marketing of higher education. The two distinct Parts have first built an argument in favour of using the tools of marketing, but in ways that help the educational values of higher education flourish. We are not sure this is or will be the case unless a more fundamental assessment of the use of marketing in higher education is undertaken and this book is intended as our contribution. Moreover, we have suggested in Part II how we might be able to harness marketing tools for the benefit of higher education.

In doing so we have suggested two main models for development of marketing higher education; at the strategic level, the CORD model developed by Felix Maringe, and at the marketing practical level, the trust-based model developed by Paul Gibbs. Together we think they can shape an approach to higher education. In this chapter we want to further develop this idea in the context of higher education and especially in relation to the ethical dimension of marketing, a constantly recurring theme in this book.

The risks of marketing higher education

The marketing literature on advertising and autonomy is extensive and concentrates on persuasive advertising, as this seems more controversial than straightforward presentation of information. Central to this literature is the seminal paper of Crisp (1987), where he offers an approach based on a model of consumers open to violation of their autonomy at the hands of manipulative copy and images. Indeed, he argues that that persuasive advertising may 'occupy the motivational territory properly belonging to the agent [consumer]' (1987: 414). He may well have a point, but his argument has no place for the advertising-literate consumer who reads the advertising verbiage for entertainment. To some extent this is Arrington's (1982) argument when he gives us four ways of understanding 'autonomy', and argues that, in each case, advertising does not violate it.

Plausible as Arrington's claims may be, Crisp's reasoning is still valid in the context of persuasion leading to actions over which the subject feels no control. In this sense advertising becomes propaganda for the vulnerable, like his example of subliminal advertising, and is violating and exploitative. Lippke's (1989) contribution is an important view of the argument when it applies to advertising. Moreover he has developed a position on advertising being exploitation based on the premise that advertising subverts and suppresses the skills, knowledge, attitudes, and motivations necessary for autonomy. Specifically with reference to advanced capitalistic economies, it does this by inducing beliefs and wants conducive to the economic and political interest of the owners of the production of the advertising and subjugates the consumer to these through advertising's control of mass media.

Not surprisingly, these wants and desire may not be 'good' in Aristotle's sense, where the 'good life' is achieved through rational happiness achieved through education of the socially situated autonomous individual, not compliance to images of satisfaction. In doing so it exploits the student as consumer by substituting their well-being for the well-being obtained though the explicit financial or ideological satisfaction of knowledge production rather than the implicit values of transformation. By linking a valued notion – liberal education – with trivial and incongruent images of hedonism, it exploits the common resources of state education by connecting it with some socio-economic valued yet educationally worthless experience. In so doing, we affect the worth of both (Jeurissen 2005). Indeed, it is to the university that we might look to develop our ability to recognize that advertising is designed to persuade us of a particular ideology of the good life and to offer us skills to decide to accept, reject or resist this or other ideologies.

It follows, we think, that if persuasive advertising is eroding educational values directly or by association, it is detrimental to the realization of autonomous educated people in the sense of their intent and action. If this proposition is valid, then it is morally dangerous to use advertising to promote the process of educating the autonomous individual through recruitment advertisements when no such education is provided. In this case such a strategy contains a contradiction and duplicity.

Moreover, if educational advertising is adopting images of mass culture, it is devaluing the authority of the university to stand back so as to question that culture. If so, it seems plausible it will maintain its own self-interest by harnessing the consumption ideology that sweeps all before it. Indeed, Adorno's (2001) and Giroux's (2004) discussion of the responsibility of education illustrates the risks that society in general runs as its universities drift towards reflecting mass culture and its marketing technologies. They have pleaded for education to face the realities of the society it is building under the architect of capitalism. The influence of the market on all areas of our economy need not be rehearsed again here. It is sufficient to point to the increased dependence of the university on sponsorships, commercial research, alumni funding, recruitment (enrolment management), endowments and encumbered government funding; even the pretence of institutional independency is being eroded in the collegiate system, to be replaced by managerialism (see Bok 2003; Kirp 2004). That Lyotard's 'dehumanization' is occurring in the very institutions once able to question society, to enable choice and to prevent the inhumanities of collective thinking is, as Waide (1987) comments, predictive of the role of advertising.

From this perspective, the notion of education is perverted by foreshortening its scope and horizons to provide trained workers and ceases to be education; it is an economic exchange that repays the workers, the students, handsomely over their lifetime. Although the economic is important, it has become a totalizing ideology that is turning education into a commodity so that it can be more readily marketed. The potential cost of this market transformation is a devaluation of liberal education's virtues of tolerance, critical thinking, trust and benevolence. The duplicity is that the advertisements offer values using the very tools the message is working against, and that this is done knowingly to increase recruitment.

We believe the university sector is facing a crisis in terms of its values as competition intensifies and, as Veloutsou et al. (2005: 279) state, institutions increasingly are 'engaging in professional marketing activities'. Furthermore Veloutsou et al.'s study concluded that the 'final chance to "sell" the goods and clinch the sale is still greatly influenced by informational sources under the direct control of the university' (2005: 289). They go further to declare that even though the content is entirely satisfactory, if it is not attractive enough – persuasive enough? – the sale will be lost. Although this is not expressed in our choice of language, the message seems all too clear; if universities don't use the promotional tool of marketing, they risk failing to recruit.

In more restrained language, Ivy (2001) argues that the image portrayed by institutions of higher education plays a critical role in how the institutions are perceived, by its stakeholders, including its competitive position with rivals. In Arpan et al.'s (2003) study of major American universities, they found that various non-academic aspects of the universities (for example, athletics) contributed highly to the universities' reputation. We are unaware of any study to look at the content of the advertising used by universities to induce positive responses, whether persuasive or just informative, but it would seem naïve to assume that persuasive advertising is not being used when UK universities recently responded to the increase of top-up fees and their need to provide bursaries by offering incentives 'either in addition to cash bursaries or as standalone offerings. For example, some students could expect to receive travel passes, laptops, vouchers for bicycles, sports centre passes and art equipment' (Office of Fair Access 2005). Returning to Veloutsou et al. (2005), one of the concerning features of their work is the distinction they draw between promotional (we assume persuasive) material and informational. The risk of exploitation seems self-evident in the competitive times facing higher education.

These are messages that, if correct, might frighten vice-chancellors or presidents into reaching for the nearest advertising agency, but what ought to concern them is the cause of this frenzy for recruitment. Who benefits? What positive impact is it having on society? What is it doing to the essence of higher education? The problem may not be inherent in the notion of advertising, but in the market mechanism. To resist both the market and its methods would require an act of defiance; one that confronted the duplicity of advertising to reduce autonomous choice while advocating a transformative process based upon the nurturing of autonomy.

Affordance of a marketing orientation

Notwithstanding the above cautionary stance, it is important to end this book by looking at the value of adopting a marketing orientation for university institutions. We reiterate our position that marketing is more than a set of functional activities such as advertising, public relations and selling. We believe that criticisms of marketing as an unethical practice, unsuited for higher education arise, in part at least, because marketing is often ordinarily associated with these activities. While they constitute important elements of marketing, they are nevertheless not its defining basis.

In this book, we define university marketing as an underlying cultural and organizational disposition to position the customer at the centre of all decisions in the critical tripartite university business of teaching, research and service. We see it as an organizational strategy aimed at creating and delivering value to its customers. Central to this mission is the need to keep customers happy regarding the way the university executes this core business. Given the importance of universities in the socio-economic and cultural development of societies, the ever-changing nature of the human and societal conditions, together with the global influences and the accelerating technological development, universities can no longer conduct their business on an *ad hoc* run-of-the-mill, short-term basis.

The need for a strategic marketing approach is not only urgent but obligatory. For two decades marketing in education has been on the march, but has been found to be inchoate (Foskett 1995; Smith et al. 1995); operational rather than strategic (Maringe 2004); poorly staffed; and removed from the core business of the university (Maringe 2005b; Helmsley-

Brown and Oplatka 2007). As higher education operates in a dynamic marketplace where competition, consumers, technology and the market forces persistently exert pressure to change, universities need to adopt a strategic marketing approach to help them look beyond the immediate circumstances into the often less well-understood future. The approach transcends the tactical and operational levels to strengthen the capacity of the institution not to only predict but plan for uncertain futures. Strategy and trust are at the heart of successful university marketing. On the one hand, we need a strategic marketing approach that sits well with the core business of universities. On the other, whatever approaches used must be trusted and held in high regard by those who operate within the university and the customers who utilize its services and products. The CORD and Trust models we suggested in this book are specifically designed to accomplish those twin challenges.

Adopting a marketing orientation is no longer an optional choice in higher education and it brings two main advantages which are briefly outlined below.

The student/customer becomes the focus of decision-making

Teaching, research and service are the core missions of universities. Despite the wide-ranging arguments to the contrary, we are firmly of the belief that the student is the most important customer of the university. A key consideration in identifying what and how to teach effectively to any group of students is to thoroughly understand the students in terms of how they learn most efficiently and how they prefer to be taught. In the 1960s, Brunner once argued that any child can be taught anything, any time, as long as the teaching is done in an honest and intellectually stimulating manner. Customers treated with honesty grow to trust the organization and the institutions that serve it. They are at the heart of key decisions of the organization. The benefits of adopting a customer orientation have been well documented in the business sector. In education, this approach becomes more relevant given the increasing involvement of students in contributing monetarily towards their higher education experience.

Issues of value for money are gradually taking centre stage in students' union charters and campaigns for the improvement of services and quality of educational provision. Thus, rather than remaining at the periphery of decision-making, students are increasingly becoming an integral part of the core business of universities. Whether it is the design of curriculum, the planning of a variety of service encounters, library and accommodation services among others, student input and views become integral to the university's decision-making and strategic planning. A customer focus will thus revolutionize the way universities conduct their core business of teaching, learning, research, and community service.

A new axis for university business

The perennial debate about the relationship between research, teaching and their relative significance in the mission of universities is based on an incompatibility theory (Baker and MacLean 2004) in which research enjoys higher status than teaching in the academic professions. However, we agree with Beyer and Liston (1996) that the separation of research from teaching presents a false dichotomy, as the two activities reinforce each other in ways that make the world more comprehensible. We would like to propose that research and teaching be viewed more broadly from a curriculum point of view, based on the understanding that the curriculum is all the experiences planned by the educational institution for the benefit of its students. Viewed that way, research and teaching are unified and become, in the words of Beyer and Liston, the centrepiece of university business. The curriculum-focused model for higher education marketing (Maringe 2004) has been developed on that basis and provides a new axis for conceptualizing and executing university business.

Glossary

aletheia	truth, truthfulness
authentic	creating and facing our life-meanings
commodification	placing more emphasis on the external rather than the intrinsic value. In education, the value approaches the price paid to obtain it
desert	deserving rather than meriting
e-learning	electronically supported learning
encashment	realizing the entity
enframed	re-shaped within a specified context and form
extended present	links past and future from the present, but within very limited time horizons
globalization	international integration
m-learning	mobile learning, i.e. using the Internet via radio connection
massification	the movement to mass participation, rather than elitism in higher education
mode 2 knowledge	socially distributed, application-oriented, transdisciplinary, and subject to multiple accountabilities
paideia	education, the process of education
phenomenology	our understanding and experience of being
phronesis	practical wisdom
poiesis	production
praxis	skilful and practical application
present-at-hand	when an object is studied in its own right
pro-educating	promotion emerging from an educational ideological education
pro-marketing	marketing emerging from an educational ideology rather than the market mechanism
psychographic	describes any attributes relating to personality, values, attitudes, interests or lifestyles
rainbow concept	a concept that has many shades of meaning and can be interpreted in a variety of ways

ready-at-hand   available for use whenever needed
techne   technical skills, historically craft skills

References

Aaker, D.A. (1998) *Strategic Market Management*. New York: Wiley Adams.

Adams, J. (2004) Higher education supply and demand to 2010: an update, in B. Bekhrandia (2007) *Evaluating and Funding Research through the Proposed Research Excellence Framework*, HEPI. Available at, www.hepi.ac.uk (accessed 14 February 2008).

Adia, E. (1996) *Higher Education: The Ethnic Minority Student Experience*. Leeds: Heist Publications.

Adorno, T.W. (2001) *The Culture Industry*. London: Routledge.

Adorno, T.W. and Horkheimer, M. (1997) *Dialectic of Enlightenment*. London: Verso Books.

Aigner, J.S., Nelson, P. and Stimpfl, J.R. (1992) *Internationalising the University: Making it Work*. Springfield, IL: CBIS Federal.

Albert, R. and Whetten, D. (1985) Organisational identity, *Research in Organisational Behaviour*, 7: 163–95.

Altbach, P. (2004) Globalisation and the university: myths and realities in an unequal World, *Tertiary Education and Management,* 10(1): 3–25.

Altbach, P.G. and Knight, J. (2006) The internationalization of higher education: motivations and realities, *Journal of Studies in International Education*, 11(3–4): 290–305.

Altbach, P.G. and McGill Peterson, P. (eds) (1999) *Higher Education in the 21st Century: Global Challenge and National Response*. Boston: Institute of International Education and Boston College Center for International Higher Education.

Alvesson, M. (1998) The business concept as a symbol, *International Studies of Management and Organisation*, 28(3): 86–108.

Aronowitz, S. (2000) *The Knowledge Factory*. Boston: Beacon Press.

Arpan, L.M., Zivnuska, A.A. and Zivnuska, S. (2003) A cognitive approach to understanding university image, *Corporate Communication: An International Journal*, 8(2): 97–113.

Arrington, R. (1982) Advertising and behavioral control, *Journal of Business Ethics*, 1: 3–12.

Ayoubi, R.M. and Massoud H.K. (2007) The strategy of internationalization in universities: a quantitative evaluation of the intent and implementation in UK universities, *International Journal of Educational Management*, 21(4): 329–49.

Baade, R.A. and Sundberg, J.O. (1996) What determines alumni generosity?, *Economics of Education Review*, 15(1): 75–81.

Bagozzi, R.P. (2000) On the concept of intentional social action in consumer behavior, *Journal of Consumer Research*, 27(3): 388–96.

Baker, H. and MacLean, M. (2004) Students making progress and the teaching research nexus debate, *Teaching in Higher Education*, 9(4): 407–19.

Ball, S.J. (1999) *Class Struggles and the Education Market*. London: Routledge Falmer.

Ball, S.J. (2004) Education for Sale! Commodification of everything? Annual Education Lecture at the Karl Mannheim Professor of Sociology of Education Institute of Education, University of London. Available at: firgoa.usc.es/drupal/node/25448 (accessed 10 January 2008).

Barker, L. (1997) Mapping the training market for individuals, in C. Robinson and R. Kenyon, *The Market for Vocational Education and Training*. Canberra: National Centre for Vocational Education Research.

Barrett, R. (2000) Market arguments and autonomy, *Journal of the Philosophy of Education*, 34(2): 327–41.

Bearden, W.O., Hardesty, D.M. and Rose, R.L. (2001) Consumer self-confidence: refinement in conceptualisation and measurement, *Journal of Consumer Research*, 28(2): 121–34.

Bell, M. (2004) *Internationalising the Higher Education Curriculum: Do Academics Agree?* Higher Education Research & Development Society of Australia, University of Wollongong, Australia.

Bennett, D. (2005) The effectiveness of current students' ambassadors in HE marketing recruitment and retention, paper presented to the International Conference on HE marketing, Cyprus, 3–5 Jan.

Beyer, L.E. and Liston, D.P. (1996) *Curriculum in Conflict: Social Visions, Educational Agendas and Progressive School Reform*. New York: Teachers College Press.

Biggs, J. (2003) *Teaching for Quality Learning at University*. Buckingham: SRNE and Open University Press.

Blake, N., Smeyers, P., Smith. R. and Standish, P. (1998) *Thinking Again: Education after Postmodernism*. Westport, CT: Bergin & Garvey.

Blumenthal, P.C., Goodwin, C.D., Smith, A. and Teichler, U. (eds) (1996) *Academic Mobility in a Changing World*. London: Jessica Kingsley Publishers.

Blythe, J. (2006) *Essentials of Marketing Management*, 3rd edn. London: Prentice Hall.

Boegh, C.A. and Tagaki, H. (2006) Internationalisation and university curricula in Denmark and Japan, *Educate*, 6(1): 25–34.

Bok, D. (2003) *Universities in the Marketplace*. Princeton NJ: Princeton, University Press.

Bologna Declaration on the European Space for HE: An explanation (2000) Confederation of EU Rectors and the Association of European Universities. Available at: ec.europa.eu/education/policies/educ/bologna/bologna.pdf (accessed 14 Feb. 2008).

Bonnett, M. (2003) Education for a post-humanist age: the question of human dwelling, *Journal of the Philosophy of Education*, 37(4): 707–24.

Borden, V. (1995) Segmenting student markets with a student satisfaction and priorities survey, *Research in Higher Education*, 36(1): 73–88.

Bottery, B. (1999) Global forces, national mediations and the management of educational institutions, *Educational Management & Administration*, 23(3): 299–312.

Bridges, D. (2006) The practice of higher education: in pursuit of excellence and of equity, *Educational Theory*, 56(4): 371–86.

Brown, S. (2001) *Marketing: The Retro Revolution*. London: Sage Publications.

Brownlie, D. and Saren, M. (1992) The four Ps of the marketing concept: prescriptive, polemical, permanent and problematic, *European Journal of Marketing*, 26(4): 34–47.

Bruner II, G.C. (1988) The marketing mix: time for a reconceptualization, *Journal of Marketing Education*, Summer: 72–7.

Buber, M. (1966) *The Knowledge of Man: A Philosophy of the Interhuman* (ed. M. S. Friedman). New York: Harper & Row.

Burstow, B. (1983) Sartre: a possible foundation for education theory, *Journal of Philosophy of Education*, 17(2): 171–85.

BUSE (Bindura University of Science Education) (2006) *Five Year Strategic Plan 2005–2006*. Bindura, Zimbabwe: BUSE.

CACI Ltd (1993) *ACORN User Guide*. London: CACI.

Campbell, F.E., Herman, R.A. and Noble, D. (2006) Contradictions in reputation management, *Journal of Communication Management*, 10(2): 191–6.

Cerny, P.G. (2003) What next for the state?, in E. Koffman and G. Young (eds) *Globalisation Theory and Practice*. London: Continuum International.

Cheney, G. and Christensen, L.T. (1999) Identity at issue: linkages between 'internal' and 'external' organisational communication, in F.M. Jablin and L.L. Putnam (eds) *New Handbook of Organisational Communication*. Newbury Park, CA: Sage Publications.

Christensen, L.T. and Askegaard, S. (2001) Corporate identity and corporate image revisited, *European Journal of Marketing*, 35(3/4): 292–315.

Christensen, L.T. and Cheney, G. (1994) Articulating identity in an organisational age, in S.A. Deetz (ed.) *Communication Yearbook*. Thousand Oaks, CA: Sage Publications, 17: 222–35.

Clarke, R. (1993) Profiling: a hidden challenge to regulation and data surveillance, *Journal of Law and Information Science*, 4(2): 403–419.

Clayson, D.E. and Haley, D.A. (2005) Marketing models in education: students as customers, products or partners, *Marketing Education Review*, 15(1): 1–10.

Clegg, S. (2003) Learning and teaching policies in higher education: mediations and contradictions of practice, *British Educational Research Journal*, 29(6): 803–19.

Coates, D. (1998) Marketing of further and higher education: an equal opportunities perspective, *Journal of Further and Higher Education*, 22(2): 135–42.

College Board (2007) Federal student aid to undergraduates shows slow growth, while published tuition prices continue to increase. Available at: www.collegeboard.com/press/releases/189547.html (accessed 15 May 2007).

Conlon, G. and Chevalier, A. (2003) Does it pay to attend a prestigious university? Discussion paper, London School of Economics, Centre for the Economics of Education (CEE).

Coughlin, C.C. and Erekson, O.H. (1985) An examination of contributions to support intercollegiate athletics, *Social Science Quarterly,* 66: 194–202.

Cranton, P. (1994) *Understanding and Promoting Transformative Learning: A Guide for Educators and Adults.* San Francisco: Jossey-Bass.

Crisp, R. (1987) Persuasive advertising, autonomy and the creation of desire, *Journal of Business Ethics,* 6: 413–18.

Curran, P.J. (2001) Competition in UK higher education: applying Porter's diamond model to geography departments, *Studies in Higher Education,* 26(2): 223–51.

Czinkota, M.R. (2004) Loosening the shackles: The future of global higher education. Available at: www.wto.org/english/tratop_e/serv_e/sym_april05_e/czinkota_education_e.doc (accessed 10 June 2007).

DAAD (German Academic Exchange Programme) (2007) *Survey and Insights into Studying Abroad.* A report for the DAAD Office, New York.

Daniels, J. (2005) Higher education for sale, portal.unesco.org/education/en/ev.php-URL_ID=7849&URL_DO=DO_TOPIC&URL_SECTION=201.html (accessed 10 June 2007).

Davies, J. (1992) Developing a strategy for internationalisation in universities: towards a conceptual framework, in C. Klasek (ed.) *Bridges to the Future: Strategies for Internationalising Higher Education.* Carbondale, IL: Association of International Education Administration, pp. 177–90.

Davies, P. (2004) *Developing a Customer Profile: Postcode Mapping using Mosaic, UK.* London: Learning and Skills Development Agency, UK.

Department for Education and Science (DfES) (2003) *The Future of Higher Education,* Government White Paper. London: HMSO. Available at: www.dfes.gov.uk/hegateway/strategy/hestrategy/index.shtml (accessed 14 Feb. 2008).

Department for Education and Science (DfES) (2004) *Increasing Voluntary Giving in Higher Education.* Available at: www.dfes.gov.uk/hegateway/uploads/Increasing%20Voluntary%20Giving%20to%20Higher%20Education%20-%20Task%20Force%20Report%20to%20Government.pdf (accessed 10 June 2007).

Department for Education and Science (DfES) (2006) *Reform of Higher Education Research Assessment and Funding: A Consultation Document.* London: HMSO.

Dewey, J. (1998) *Experience and Education: The 60th Anniversary Edition.* West Lafayette, IN: Kappa Delta Pi.

Ditcher, S.F. (1985) The organization of the '90s, *The McKinsey Quarterly*, 1: 145–55.

Doti, J. (2004) Is higher education becoming a commodity?, *Journal of Higher Education Policy and Management*, 26(3): 363–9.

Dove, K.E. (2001) *Conducting a Successful Fundraising Program*. San Francisco: Jossey-Bass.

Doyle, J.L. (1998) Class, consumerism and education, *International Journal of Educational Management*, 12(4): 183–7.

Doyle, P. (2002) *Marketing Management and Strategy*. London: Prentice Hall.

Doyle, P. and Stern, P. 2006 *Marketing Management and Strategy*. London: Financial Times/Prentice Hall.

Drucker, P. (1954) *The Practice of Management*. New York: Harper & Row.

Drucker, P. (1973) *Management: Tasks, Responsibilities and Practices*. London: Harper & Row.

Drummond, G. (2004) Consumer confusion: reduction strategies in higher education, *International Journal of Educational Management*, 18(5): 317–23.

Drummond, G. and Ensor, J. (2003) *Strategic Marketing, Planning and Control*. Oxford: Butterworths.

DSS Research, Choice modelling for decisive results. Available at: www.dssresearch.com (accessed 14 Feb. 2008).

Duncan, J.G. (1989) Marketing of higher education: problems and issues in theory and practice, *Higher Education Quarterly*, 43(2): 175–88.

Dutton, J.E., Dukerich, J.M and Harquail, C.V. (1994) Organizational images and member identification: sustainable competitive advantage, *Journal of Management*, 17: 191–206.

Eagle, L. and Brennan, R. (2007) Are students customers? TQM and marketing perspectives, *Quality Assurance in Education*, 15(1): 44–60.

Everett, J. and Armstrong, R. (1993) A case study of MBA market in Western Australia, *Journal of Marketing for Higher Education*, 4(1–2): 309–23.

Farr, M. (2002) Measuring participation in higher education using geodemographics. Unpublished PhD thesis, University of Lancaster.

Farr, M. (2003a) Extending participation in higher education: an investigation into applicant choice using postcode analysis. Unpublished dissertation, Lancaster University.

Farr, M. (2003b) Educational Mosaic; Combining the new census with learner data to develop a postcode classification, LSDA, UCAS and higher education adapts.

Featherstone, M. (1991) *Consumer Culture and Postmodernism.* London: Sage.

Fill, C. (2006) *Marketing Communications.* London: Financial Times Press.

Financial Times (2006) Reputation: you only know what it is when it lies in tatters, 3 March.

Fitzsimons, P. (2002) Enframing education, in M. Peters (ed.) *Heidegger, Education and Modernity.* Lanham, MD: Rowman & Littlefield Publishers, pp. 171–90.

Foskett, N. (1995) Marketing management and schools: a study of developing marketing culture in secondary schools. Unpublished PhD thesis, University of Southampton.

Foskett, N., Dyke, M. and Maringe, F. (2004) *The Influence of the School in the Decision to Participate in Learning Post 16.* DfES Research Report No. 538. London: DfES.

Foskett, N. and Helmsley-Brown, J. (2001) *Choosing Futures: Young People's Decision Making in Education, Training and Career Markets.* London: Routledge Falmer.

Foskett, N., Maringe, F. and Roberts, D. (2006) *Changing Fee Regimes and their Impact on Student Attitudes to Higher Education.* York: Higher Education Academy.

Foxall, G.R. (1998) Intention versus context in consumer psychology, *Journal of Marketing*, 14: 29–62.

Freire, P. (1970) *Pedagogy of the Oppressed*, trans. M.B. Ramos. New York: Continuum.

Further Education Funding Council for England (FEFCE) (1998) *Marketing: A Good Practice Guide.* London: The Stationery Office.

Gadamer, H-G. (1975) *Truth and Method*, trans. G. Berden and J. Cummings. New York: Seabury Press.

Gerson, R.F. (1993) *Measuring Customer Satisfaction.* London: Kogan Page.

Gibbons, M., Limoges, C., Nowotny, H., Schwartzman, S., Scott, P. and Trow, M. (1994) *The New Production of Scientific Knowledge: The Dynamics of Science and Research in Contemporary Societies.* London: Sage.

Gibbs, P. (1998) Time, temporality and consumer behaviour: a review of the literature and implications for certain financial services, *European Journal of Marketing*, 32: 993–1007.

Gibbs, P. (2002) From the invisible hand to the invisible handshake: marketing higher education, *Research in Post/Higher Education*, 7(3): 323–35.

Gibbs, P. (2007) Does advertising pervert higher education? The case for resistance, *Journal of the Marketing of Higher Education*, 17(1): 3–11.

Giddens, A. (1991) *Modernity and Self-Identity*. Cambridge: Polity Press.

Giroux, H.A. (2004) Education after Abu Ghraib, *Cultural Studies*, 18(6): 779–815.

Goldghein, L.A. and Kane, K.L. (1997) Repositioning the MBA: issues and implications, *Journal of Marketing for Higher Education*, 8(1): 15–24.

Gottfried, M.A. and Johnson, E.L. (2005) Solicitation and donation: An econometric evaluation of alumni generosity in higher education, *International Journal of Educational Advancement*, 6(94): 268–81.

Graeves, A. (2004) *Developing a Customer Profile: Approaches to Segmentation*. London: Learning and Skills Council, UK.

Gray, L. (1991) *Education Marketing*. Buckingham: Open University Press.

Greenfield, J.M. (2002) *Fundraising Fundamentals*. San Francisco: Jossey-Bass.

Greyser, S. (1996) Corporate reputation and the bottom line. Unpublished address given at the launch of the International Corporate Identity Group, House of Lords, London, 24 January.

Grimes, P.W. and Chressanthis, G.A. (1994) Alumni contributions to academics: the role of intercollegiate sports and NCAA sanctions, *American Journal of Economics and Sociology*, 53: 27–40.

Habermas, J. (1984) *The Theory of Communicative Action*. Cambridge: Polity Press.

Habermas, J. (1998) *The Philosophical Discourse of Modernity*, trans. F. Lawrence. Cambridge: Polity Press.

Hassan, R. (2003) *The Chronoscopic Society: Globalization, Time and Knowledge in the Network Economy*. Oxford: Peter Lang.

Hayward, D.M. and Elliott, C.S. (1998) The expanding definition of framing and its particular impact on economic experimentation, *Journal of Public Relations Research*, 11(3): 205–42.

Heidegger, M. (1962) *Being and Time*. Oxford: Blackwell.

Heidegger, M. (1977) *The Question Concerning Technology and Other Essays*. New York: Harper & Row.

Heidegger, M. (1978) Building, dwelling, thinking, in *Basic Writings*, trans. D. F. Krell. London: Routledge, pp. 343–436.

Heidegger, M. (2000) Letter on humanism, in *Basic Writings*. New York: Harper & Row.

Helmsley-Brown, J. (1996) Marketing post-sixteen colleges: a qualitative and quantitative study of pupils' choice of post-sixteen institution, unpublished PhD thesis, University of Southampton.

Helmsley-Brown, J. and Oplatka, I. (2007) Universities in a competitive global marketplace: a systematic review of the literature on higher education marketing, *International Journal of Public Sector Management*, 19(4): 292–305.

Hesketh, A.J. and Knight, P.T. (1999) Postgraduates' choice of programme: helping universities to market and postgraduates to choose, *Studies in Higher Education*, 24(2): 151–63.

Higher Education Funding Council for England (HEFCE) (2000) Diversity in higher education. HEFCE policy statement.

Higher Education Statistical Agency (HESA) (2005–06) Students in Higher Education institutions. Available at: www.hesa.ac.uk/index.php?option=com_datatables&Itemid=121&task=show_category&catdex=3 (accessed 14 February 2008).

Hirsch, R. (1976) *Social Limits to Growth*. Cambridge, MA: Harvard University Press.

Hirschman, E.C. (1986) Humanistic enquiry in marketing research: philosophy, method and criteria, *Journal of Marketing Research*, 23: 237–49.

Holt, D.B. (1997) Poststructuralist lifestyle analysis: conceptualizing the social patterning of consumption in post modernity, *Journal of Consumer Research*, 23 March: 326–50.

Huang, F. (2007) Internationalization of higher education in the developing and emerging countries, *Journal of Studies in International Education*, 11: 421–32.

Huisman, J. and van der Wende, M.C. (eds) (2004) *On Cooperation and Competition: National and European Policies for Internationalisation of Higher Education*. ACA Papers on International Cooperation. Bonn: Lemmens.

Hutton, J.G. (1999) The definition, dimensions and domains of public relations, *Public Relations Review*, 25(2): 199–214.

Ind, N. (1992) *The Corporate Image: Strategies for Effective Identity Programmes.* London: Kogan Page.

Ivy, J. (2001) Higher education institution image: a correspondence analysis approach, *The International Journal of Educational Management*, 15(6): 276–82.

Ivy, J. (2002) University image: the role of marketing in MBA student recruitment in state-subsidised universities in the Republic of South Africa. Unpublished PhD thesis, University of Leicester.

James, R., Baldwin, G. and McInnis, C. (1999) *Which University? The Factors Influencing Choices of Prospective Undergraduates.* Evaluation and Investigations programme, Higher Education Division, Australia.

Janic, Z. and Zabber, V. (2002) Impersonal vs personal exchanges in marketing relationships, *Journal of Marketing Management*, 18(7/8): 657–71.

Jeurissen, R (2005) Is marketing exploitative? Institute of Ethical Business Worldwide, Notre Dame University, IN. Available at: www.ethicalbusiness.nd.edu/events/Marketing%20Ethics%   20Workshop/ conferencePapers.htm (accessed 20 December. 2005).

Johnston, J. and Edelstein, R. (1993) *Beyond Borders: Profiles of International Education.* Washington, DC: Association of American Colleges.

Kenway, J. with Bigum, C. and Fitzclarence, L. (1993) Marketing education in the postmodern age, *Journal of Education Policy*, 8(2): 105–22.

Kirp, D.L. (2004) *Shakespeare, Einstein and the Bottom Line.* Cambridge, MA: Harvard University Press.

Knight, J. (1995) Internationalisation of higher education: conceptual framework, in J. Knight and H. de Wit (eds) *Internationalisation of Higher Education in Asia Pacific Countries.* Amsterdam: European Association for International Education Publications.

Knight, J. (1999) Internationalisation of higher education in IMHE, in *Quality & Internationalisation in Higher Education,* Paris: OECD.

Knight, J. (2003) Updating the definition of internationalisation, *International Higher Education*, 33: 2–3.

Knight, J. and de Wit, H. (1995) *Internationalisation of Higher Education in Asia Pacific Countries.* Amsterdam: EAIE.

Kotler, P. (1987) Humanistic marketing: beyond the marketing concept, in A.F. Firat, N. Dholakia and R.P. Bagozzi (eds) *Philosophical and Radical Thought in Marketing.* Lexington, MA: Lexington Books.

Kotler, P. (1998) *Marketing Management: Analysis, Planning, Implementation and Control.* Englewood Cliffs, NJ: Prentice Hall.

Kotler, P. (2005) *Marketing Management*, 11th edn. New Delhi: Pearson Education.

Lafferty, B.A. and Hult, G.T.M. (2001) A synthesis of contemporary market orientation perspectives, *European Journal of Marketing*, 35(1/2): 92–109.

Lambert Review (2003) *Business University Collaboration.* London: HMSO.

Lauder, H. and Lauder, D. (1999) *Trading in Future: Why Markets in Education Don't Work.* Buckingham and Philadelphia: Open University Press.

Lawlor, J. (2007) Intelligent marketing solutions for education. Available at: at www.tlg.com

Learndirect (2003) *Understanding the Adult Learner Market: Segmenting the Market According to Attitudes to Learning.* Research Summary Series of Learndirect UFI.

Leslie, L.L. and Ramey, G. (1988) Donor behavior and voluntary support for higher education institutions, *Journal of Higher Education*, 59: 115–32.

Levitt, T. (1974) Innovative imitation, *Harvard Business Review*, 44(5): 63–71.

Li, F. and Nicholls, J.A.F. (2000) Transactional or relational marketing: determinants of strategic choices, *Journal of Marketing Management*, 16(5): 449–64.

Lippke, R.L. (1989) Advertising and the social conditions of autonomy, *Business and Professional Ethics Journal*, 8: 35–58.

Lipsett, A. (2005) 'Customer' students to call tune, *Times Higher Education Supplement* (Issue 1717), 11 November.

Litten, L.H. (1991) Ivy bound: high ability students and college choice, *US Today*.

Little, M.W., O'Toole, D.O. and Wetzel, J. (1997) The price differentials; impact on retention, recruitment and quality in a public university, *Journal of Marketing for Higher Education*, 8(2): 37–51.

Liu, S.S. (1998) Integrating strategic marketing on an institutional level, *Journal of Marketing for Higher Education*, 8(4): 17–28.

Lobkowicz, N. (1983) Man, the pursuit of truth and the university, in J.W. Chapman (ed.) *The Western University on Trial.* Berkeley, CA: University of California Press, pp. 27–39.

Luhmann, N. (1979) *Trust and Power.* Chichester: John Wiley & Sons, Ltd.

Lumby, J., Foskett, N. and Maringe, F. (2004) Pathways and progression on 16, Fashion, Peer Influence and College Choice, paper presented at BERA Conference, September 2004.

Lynch, K. (1997) A profile of mature students in higher education and an analysis of equality issues. Available at: www.ucc.ie/publications/heeu/ Mature/mature_8.htm (accessed 11 April 2005).

Maguire, M., Ball, S.J. and Macrae, S. (1999) Promotion, persuasion and class-taste; marketing (in) the UK post-compulsory sector, *British Journal of Sociology of Education*, 20(3): 291–308.

Manger, P. (2006) Maybe dolphins aren't so smart after all, scientist suggests, 10.12pm *ET CBC News*, 19 August.

Margison, S. (2004) National and global competition in higher education, *The Australian Educational Researcher*, 31(2): 1–28.

Margulies, W. (1997) Make the most of your corporate identity, *Harvard Business Review*, July/August: 66–72.

Maringe, F. (2004) Marketing university education: an investigation into the perceptions, practices and prospects of university marketing in Zimbabwe. Unpublished PhD thesis, University of Southampton.

Maringe, F. (2005a) Interrogating the crisis in Higher Education marketing: the CORD model, *International Journal of Educational Management*, 19(7): 564–78.

Maringe, F. (2005b) University marketing: perceptions, practices and prospects in the less developed world, *Journal of Marketing for Higher Education*, 15(2): 129–53.

Maringe, F. (2006) University and course choice: implications for positioning, recruitment and marketing, *International Journal of Educational Management*, 20(6–7): 466–97.

Maringe, F. (2007) Diversification of post-graduate students' recruitment markets: opportunities for science and mathematics PGCE recruitment, *Higher Education Review*, 39(2): 43–64.

Maringe, F. and Carter, S. (2007) International students' motivations for studying in UK Higher Education: insights into the choice and decision making of African students, *International Journal of Educational Management*, 21(6): 459–75.

Maringe, F. and Foskett, N. (2002) Marketing university education: the Southern African experience, *Higher Education Review*, 34(3): 35–51.

Mazzarol, T. (1999) An examination of the factors critical to the establishment and maintenance of competitive advantage for education services enterprises within international markets. Unpublished PhD thesis, Curtin University of Technology.

Mazzarol, T., Soutar, G.N. and Thein, V. (2000) Critical success factors in the marketing of an education institution: a comparison of institutional and student perspectives, *Journal of Marketing for Higher Education*, 10(2): 39–57.

McInnis, C. (1998) Academics and professional administrators in Australian universities: dissolving boundaries and new tensions, *Journal of Higher Education Policy and Management*, 20(2): 161–73.

McLeod, O. (1999) Desert and institutions, in O. McLeod and L. Pojman. (eds) What Do We Deserve? Oxford: Oxford University Press.

McMurty, J. (1991) Education and the market model, *Journal of the Philosophy of Education*, 25(2): 209–18.

Meek, V.L. (2000) Diversity and the marketisation of higher education: incompatible concepts?, *Higher Education Policy*, 13: 23–39.

Mezirow, J. (1997) Transformative learning: theory to practice, in P. Cranton (ed.) *Transformative Learining in Action: Insights from Practice*. San Francisco: Jossey-Bass.

Miaoulis, G. and Kalfus, D. (1983) Ten MBA benefit segments, *Marketing News*, 5 August.

Miller, P., Lamb, C.W., Jr., Hoverstad, R. and Boehm, E.G. (1990) An approach for identifying benefit segments among prospective college students, *Journal of Marketing for Higher Education*, 3(1): 49–65.

Mintzberg, H. (1996) Managing government, governing management, *Harvard Business Review*, May/June: 75–83.

Moloney, K. (2000) *Rethinking Public Relations: The Spin and the Substance*. London: Routledge.

Moore, J.C. (ed.) (2005) *Engaging Communities: Wisdom from the Sloan Consortium*. Elements of Quality of Online Education, Sloan-Consortium.

Mugabe, R. (2004) Too little too late. Mugabe mocks the Commonwealth, *The Guardian*, 3 March.

Muniz, Jr., A.M. and O'Gunn, T.C. (2001) Brand communities, *Journal of Consumer Research*, 27 (March): 412–33.

Murphy, P.E. and Staples, W. (1979) A modernised family life cycle, *Journal of Consumer Research*, June.

Naidoo, R. (2007) HE as a global commodity, Observatory on Borderless Higher Education. Available at: www.obhe.ac.uk (accessed 14 February 2008).

Naidoo, R. and Jamieson, I. (2005) Empowering participants or corroding learning? Towards a research agenda on the impact of student consumerism in higher education, *Journal of Education Policy*, 20(3): 267–81.

National Student Survey (2005) Summary report. Available at: http://www.hefce.ac.uk/pubs/rdreports/2007/rd14_07/ (accessed 29 April 2008).

Naude, P. and Ivy, J. (1999) Marketing strategies of universities in the United Kingdom, *The International Journal of Educational Management*, 13(3): 126–34.

Nentwich, M. (2001) (Re-)De-commoditisation in academic knowledge distribution?, *Science Studies*, 14(2): 21–42.

Nowotny, H. (1988) From the future to the extended present, in G. Kirsch, P. Nijkamp and K. Zimmermann (eds) *A Multidisciplinary Perspective*. Aldershot: Avery.

Nowotny, H., Scott, P. and Gibbons, M. (2001) *Rethinking Science: Knowledge and the Public in an Age of Uncertainty*. Cambridge: Polity Press.

Office for Fair Access (OFFA) (2005) Hundreds of thousands of students from low income backgrounds set to benefit from over £300 million extra 'free cash' set aside by universities and colleges. Available at: www.offa.org.uk/news/2005/acc_agr.as, press release, 17 March.

Office for Fair Access (OFFA) (2006) Annual Report. Available at: www.offa.org.uk/wp-content/uploads/2006/07/06_01.pdf (accessed 14 February 2008).

Office for Fair Access (OFFA) (2007) www.offa.org.uk/wp-content/uploads/2007/02/1% 20 Feb%2007%20OFFA%20Ipsos%20MORI%20good%20practice%20guidance1.pdf, p. 26 (accessed 1 August 2007).

Office for Fair Access (OFFA) (2008) www.offa.org.uk/access-agreements/basics (accessed 14 Feb 2008).

Opinion Panel (2007) How much would students pay? Available at: www.opinionpanel.co.uk/students/newsDetail.cfm?newsId=62 (accessed 12 May 2007).

Organisation for Economic Co-operation and Development (OECD) (2000) *Education at a Glance, OECD Indicators*. Paris: OECD Publications.

Organisation for Economic Cooperation and Development (OECD) (2007) *Education at a Glance: OECD Indicators*. Paris: OECD Publishing.

O'Shaughnessy, J. and O'Shaughnessy, N.J. (2007) Reply to criticisms of marketing, the consumer society and hedonism, *European Journal of Marketing*, 41(1/2): 7–16.

Oster, S.M. (2001) The effect of university endowment growth on giving: is there evidence of crowding out? Paper presented at Cornell Research Conference 'Financing Higher Education Institutions in the 21st Century', May: 1–29.

Parasuraman, A. (1991) *Marketing Research*. Reading, MA: Addison-Wesley Publishing Company.

Peattie, S. and Peattie, K. (2003) Ready to fly solo? Reducing social marketing's dependence on commercial marketing theory, *Marketing Theory*, 3(3): 365–86.

Pinch, S., Henry, N., Jenkins, M. and Tallmen, S. (2003) From industrial districts to knowledge clusters: a model of knowledge dissemination and competitive advantage in industrial agglomerations, *Journal of Economic Geography*, 3: 373–88.

Porter, M. (1990) The competitive advantage of nations, *Harvard Business Review*, 68(2) (March–April).

Porter, M. (1998) *Competitive Advantage: Techniques for Analysing Industries and Competitors*. New York: The Free Press.

Pounder. J.S. (2000) Examining the competing values frameworks in higher educational context: implications of a Hong Kong study, *International Journal of Management and Decision Making*, 1(1): 103–19.

Push, www.push.co.uk (accessed 10 Aug. 2007).

Qiang, Z. (2003) Internationalisation of HE: towards a conceptual framework, *Policy Futures in Education*, 1(2): 248–70.

Rawlinson, P. (2005) *Market Segmentation*. London: Learning and Skills Council, UK.

Rawls, J. (1991) *A Theory of Justice*. Oxford: Oxford University Press.

Read, P., Higgs, G. and Taylor, G. (2005) The potential barriers to the use of geographical information systems for marketing applications in higher education systems, *Marketing Intelligence & Planning*, 23(1): 30–42.

Readings, B. (1997) *The University in Ruins*. Cambridge, MA: Harvard University Press.

Reisman, D., Glazer, N. and Denney, R. (1950) *The Lonely Crowd*. New Haven, CT: Yale University Press.

Research Councils UK (RCUK) (2007) *Researchers: What is the Situation?* Annual Report, Swindon: RCUK.

Rhoads, T.A. and Gerking, S. (2000) Educational contributions, academic quality, and athletic success, *Contemporary Economic Policy*, 18: 248–58.

Richins, M.L. (1994) Special possessions and the expression of material values, *Journal of Consumer Research*, 21 (Dec.): 522–33.

Robbins, L. (1963) *Higher Education Report: Report of a Committee Chaired by Lord Robbins*. Cmnd 2154. London: HMSO.

Roberts, D. (1998) *Student Horizons: The Class of 1998*. Leeds: Heist.

Roberts, D. (1999) *The Marketing of Vocational Part Time Higher Education*. Leeds: Heist.

Roberts, D. and Maringe, F. (2005) Market segmentation: meanings, rationale, strategies and implications for university positioning, part of a consultation project led by The Knowledge Partnership, Staffordshire University, May.

Robertson, S., Bonal, X. and Dale, R. (2002) GATS and the education service industry, *Comparative Education Review*, 46(4): 472–97.

Robertson, S. and Dale, R. (2002) Local states of emergency: the contradictions of neo-liberal governance in education in New Zealand, *British Journal of Sociology of Education*, 23(3): 463–82.

Robson, C. (1993) *Real World Research: A Resource for Social Scientists and Practitioners-Researchers*. Oxford: Blackwell.

Rodgers, G., Finley, D. and Kline, T. (2001) Understanding individual differences in university undergraduates: a learner needs segmentation approach, *Innovative Higher Education*, 25(3): 183–96.

Rose, D. and O'Reilly, K. (eds) (1999) *Constructing Class: Towards a New Social Classification for England*. ESRC/ONS.

Ross Group (2007) Increasing voluntary giving to higher education. Available at: www.universitiesuk.ac.uk/consultations/responses/downloads/voluntary.pdf (accessed 24 April 2008).

Ryan, Y. (2002) Emerging indicators of success and failure in borderless higher education: a report for the Observatory on Borderless Higher Education, London. Available at: www.obhe.ac.uk/products/reports/Price%20List%20-%20Reports.pdf (accessed 14 February 2008).

Sartre, J-P. (1990) *Being and Nothingness*, trans. H. Barnes. Englewood Cliffs, NJ: Prentice Hall.

Scott, D., Brown, A., Lunt, I. and Thorne, L. (2004) *Professional Doctorates: Integrating Professional and Academic Knowledge.* Milton Keynes: Open University Press.

Scott, P. (2004) Ethics 'in' and 'for' Higher Education, paper presented at International Conference on Ethical and Moral Dimensions for Higher Education and Science in Europe. Available at: www.cepes.ro/September/ introduction.htm (accessed 23 July 2007).

Scott, R.A. (1992) *Campus Developments in Response to the Challenges of Internationalisation: The Case of Ramapo College of New Jersey (USA).* Springfield, IL: CBIS Federal.

Scott, S.V. (1999) The academic service provider: Is the customer always right?, *Journal of Higher Education Policy and Management,* 21(2): 193–203.

Sharrock, G. (2000) Why students are not just customers, and other reflections on life after George, *Journal of Higher Education and Policy and Management,* 22(2): 149–64.

Shaw, K.E. (2005) Researching the trade in knowledge between the West and developing countries, *International Journal of Educational Management,* 19(6): 459–68.

Simpson. L.C. (1995) *Technology, Time and the Conversation of Modernity.* London: Routledge.

Slattery, P. (1995) A postmodern vision of time and learning: a response to the National Education Commission Report 'Prisoners of Time', *Harvard Education Review,* 65(4): 612–33.

Smith, A. ([1776] 1993) *The Wealth of Nations: Inquiry into the Nature and Causes of the Wealth of Nations.* London: Hackett Publishing Co.

Smith, D., Scott, P. and Lynch, J. (1995) *The Role of Marketing in the University and College Sector.* Leeds: Heist Publication.

Soutar, G. and Turner, J. (2002) Students' preferences for university: a conjoint analysis, *The International Journal of Educational Management,* 16(1): 40–5.

Standish, P. (1997) Heidegger and the technology of further education, *Journal of the Philosophy of Education,* 31: 439–59.

Stewart, D.M. (1999) The meaning of merit, *American Behavioral Scientist,* 42(6): 1052–63.

Survey of Gift Revenue and Costs (2006) Available at: www.case.org/Content/ CASEEurope/Display.cfm?contentItemID=6610 (accessed 10 July 2007).

Sutton Trust (2006) University funding: An update. Available at: http://www.suttontrust.com/reports/UniversityFundraisingDec06.pdf (accessed 12 Feb. 2008).

Symes, C. (1998) Education for sale: a semiotic and analysis of school prospectuses and other forms of educational marketing, *Studies in Higher Education*, 42(2): 133–52.

Thiede, V. (1998) Establishing a Marketing Department at the India University Foundation, quoted in Dove, 2001.

Thompson, C.J. (1997) Interpreting consumers: a hermeneutical framework for deriving marketing insights from the texts of consumers' consumption stories, *Journal of Marketing Research*, XXXIV (November): 438–55.

Thurstone, L.L. (1931) Measurement of social attitudes, *Journal of Abnormal and Social Psychology*, 26: 249–69.

Tomer, J.F. (1998) Beyond transaction markets, toward relationship marketing in the human firm: a socio-economic model, *Journal of Socio-Economics*, 27(2): 207–28.

Tonks, D.G. and Farr, M.W. (1995) Market segments for higher education, *Market Intelligence and Planning*, 13(4): 24–33.

Tyler, R.W. (1949) *Basic Principles of Curriculum and Instruction*. Chicago: University of Chicago Press.

Tysome, T. (2006) Conference paper, Society for Research into Higher Education, UK.

UKCOSA (2004) *Broadening our Horizons: International Students in UK Universities and Colleges: Report of UKCOSA survey 2004, in Conjunction with the British Council, UUK and the Standing Committee of Principals*. London: UKCOSA.

United Nations Economic Commission for Africa (UNECA) (2000) *Aide Memoir: Report of the Regional Conference on Brain Drain and Capacity Building in Africa*. Addis Ababa, 22–24 February.

United Nations Educational Scientific and Cultural Organisation (UNESCO) (1998) World Declaration on Higher Education. Available at: www.unesco.org/education/educprog/wche/declaration_eng.htm (accessed 14 February 2008).

United Nations Educational Scientific and Cultural Organisation (UNESCO) (2002) Higher Education for Sale. Available at: portal.unesco.org/education/en/ev.php-URL_ID=7849&URL_DO=DO_TOPIC&URL_SECTION=201.html (accessed 10 June 2007).

UNESCO/USIS/OECD (2003) *Financing Education Investments and Returns: Analysis of the World Education Indicators*. Paris: UNESCO/OECD.

Universities UK (UUK) (2004/05) *Annual Review*. London: UUK.

US and World Report (2003) *America's Best Graduate Schools: Directories of Institutions and Programs*. Washington, DC: US Department of Education.

van der Wende, M. (1997) Missing links: the relationship between national policies for internationalisation and those for higher education in general, in T. Kalvermark and M. van der Wende (eds) *National Policies for the Internationalisation of Higher Education in Europe*. Stockholm: Högskoleverket.

Vandermerwe, S. and L'Huillier, M. (1989) Euro consumers in 1992, *Business Horizons*, Jan.–Feb.: 34–40.

Veloutsou, C., Paton, R.A. and Lewis, J. (2005) Consultation and the reliability of information sources pertaining to university section, *International Journal of Educational Management*, 19(4): 279–91.

Vickers, P. and Bekhradnia, B. (2007) *The Economic Costs and Benefits of International Students*. London: Higher Education Policy Institute, HEPI.

Vincent-Lancrin, S. (2004) Building future scenarios for universities and higher education: an international approach, *Policy Futures in Education*, 2(2): 245–62.

Waide, J. (1987) The making of self and the world in advertising, *Journal of Business Ethics*, 6: 73–9.

Walton, J. (2005) Would the real corporate university please stand up?, *Journal of European and Industrial Training*, 29(1): 7–20.

Warner, G. (1992) Internationalisation models and the role of the university, *International Education Magazine*, 21.

Wasmer, D.J., Williams, J.R. and Stevenson, J. (1997) A reconceptionalization of the marketing mix: using the 4 Cs to improve marketing planning in higher education, *Journal of Marketing for Higher Education*, 8(2): 29–35.

Waterhouse, R. (2002) Serve the customer, *Times Higher Education Supplement*, 20 Dec. (Issue 1569): 14.

Wilcox, J.R. and Ebbs, S.L. (1992) Promoting an ethical campus climate: the values audit, *NASPA Journal*, 29(4): 253–60.

Williams, G. (1997) The market route to mass higher education: British experience 1979–1996, *Higher Education Policy*, 10(3/4): 275–89.

Willmott, H. (1995) Managing the academics: commodification and control in the development of university education in the UK, *Human Relations*, 48(9): 993–1027.

Willmott, H. (2003) Commercialising higher education in the UK: the state, industry and peer review, *Studies in Higher Education*, 28(2): 129–41.

Wilson, R. and Gilligan, C. (2002) *Strategic Marketing Management: Planning Implementation and Control*. London: Butterworth.

Yang, R. (2002) University internationalisation, its meanings, rationales and implications, *Intercultural Education*, 13(1): 81–99.

Yeatman, A. (1993) The politics of post-matrimonial governance, in T. Seddon and L. Angus (eds) (2000) Australian Council for Educational Research Australia.

Ylijoki, O.-H. and Mäntylä, H. 2003 Conflicting time perspectives in academic work, *Time & Society*, 12(1): 55–78.

Young, J. (2002) *Heidegger's Later Philosophy*. Cambridge: Cambridge University Press.

Zineldin, M. (1988) Towards an ecological strategic business relationship management: 'A co-operative perspective', *European Journal of Marketing*, 32(11/12): 1138–64.

INDEX

SUSTAINING CHANGE IN UNIVERSITIES
Continuities in case studies and concepts

Burton R. Clark

University of California, Los Angeles, USA

- What can be done to ensure universities are well positioned to meet the challenges of the fast moving world of the 21st century?

This is the central question addressed by Burton R. Clark in this significant new volume which greatly extends the case studies and concepts presented in his 1998 book, *Creating Entrepreneurial Universities*. The new volume draws on case studies of fourteen proactive institutions in the UK, Europe, Australia, Latin America, Africa, and the United States that extend analysis into the early years of the twenty-first century. The cumulative international coverage underpins a more fully developed conceptual framework offering insight into ways of initiating and sustaining change in universities.

This new conceptual framework shifts attention from transformation to sustainability rooted in a constructed steady state of change and a collegial approach to entrepreneurialism. It contains key elements necessary for universities to adapt successfully to the modern world.

Lessons for reform can be drawn directly from both the individual case studies and the general framework. Overall the book offers a new form of university organization that is more self-reliant and manages to combine change with continuity, traditional academic values with new managerial values.

Essential reading for university administrators, faculty members, students and researchers analysing higher education, and educational policymakers worldwide, this book advocates a highly proactive approach to university change and specifies a new basis for university self reliance.

Contents

Part 1: Sustaining Entrepreneurialism in European Universities – *Introduction – Sustainability at Warwick: A paradigmatic case -Strathclyde: Sustaining change in a place of useful learning – University of Twente: Balancing on entrepreneurial seesaws in a Dutch university – University of Joensuu: Balancing sustainability in a regional Finnish university – Chalmers University of Technology: Entrepreneurialism redeemed – From transformation to sustainability – **Part 2: Amplifying Variations in University Entrepreneurialism: Africa, Latin America, Asia, North America** – Introduction – Makerere University: Entrepreneurial rebound from academic pits in Uganda – The Catholic University of Chile: Lessons from South America – Monash University: Seizing the revolutionary moment in Australia – Genetic entrepreneurialism among American universities Stanford; Massachusetts Institute of Technology; University of Michigan; University of California, Los Angeles; North Carolina State University; Georgia Institute of Technology; conclusion – **Part 3: The Self-Reliant University** – The entrepreneurial road to university self-reliance: – Why many universities will not become entrepreneurial; Key features of entrepreneurial organization in universities; The modern pathway to university autonomy and self-reliance – Notes and References – Index.*

September 2004 232pp

978 0 335 21590 4 Paperback

978 0 335 21591 1 Hardback

Managing Successful Universities

Michael Shattock

"Michael Shattock is the master craftsman of sturdy self-reliance in modern public universities. Knowing that ministerial steering will not, can not, do the job in the twenty-first century, he charts an alternative course for continuous change. His liberating lessons will be useful not only in Britain but around the world."

Professor Burton R. Clark, University of California, Los Angeles

"What do we mean by a successful university? How is such success measured? Are our criteria for success consistent with maintaining and enhancing diversity of mission? How can decline be avoided and failure redressed? And what forms of university management are most appropriate to stimulating success?Few people are better qualified by experience and by scholarship to ask and to answer such questions than Michael Shattock ...this important new book strengthens the argument for seeing good management as a necessary condition for effective and worthwhile teaching, learning and research, and its neglect as a serious threat to core academic values."

Professor Sir William Taylor, Former Director, University of London Institute of Education

"Michael Shattock is without doubt Britain's leading authority on the dangerously neglected subject of university management ...For some his book will not make comfortable reading." Professor Geoffrey Alderman, Vice-President, American InterContinental University, London

This book defines good management in a university context and how it can contribute to university success. It emphasizes the holistic characteristics of university management, the need to be outward looking and entrepreneurial in management style, the importance of maintaining a strong academic/administrative partnership and a continuous dialogue between the centre and academic departments, and the preservation of a self-directed institutional autonomy. It draws on the literature of management in the private sector as well as from higher education, and from the experience of the author. *Managing Successful Universities* demonstrates how successful universities utilise the market to reinforce academic excellence.

Contents: Introduction – What are the characteristics of a successful university? – Strategic management in universities – Managing university finance – The academic context: Organization, collegiality and leadership – Good governance – Extending the boundaries – Building an image, establishing a reputation – Ambition – Inhibitions to becoming entrepreneurial – Turning round failure or arresting decline – Managing universities for success – Appendix – References – Index.

2003 216pp

978 0 335 20961 3 Paperback

978 0 335 20962 0 Hardback

Managing Institutional Self-Study

David Watson and Elizabeth Maddison

- What is institutional self-study and why is it important for universities and colleges?
- What are its key processes and techniques?
- What can self-study offer institutions for their future success?

Organizational learning is a key concept for complex enterprises at the start of the 21st century and universities and colleges are no exception. However many institutions have been poor at recognising, reacting to and resolving dilemmas raised by changing public and political expectations. This book offers practical guidance, set in the context of theory and with worked examples, showing how disciplined self-study underpins the key decision-making, institutional processes. Moreover, the examples demonstrate that self-study supports the general effectiveness of universities and colleges and leads to improved reputational positioning.

At the heart of the book is the case for the development of the university or college as a mature, self-reflective community, capable of making full use of its analytical and other resources, thereby meeting the internal drive towards evidence-based practice and satisfying the requirements of external agencies.

Managing Institutional Self-Study is essential reading for higher education managers and policy-makers.

Contents: List of figures and tables – Foreword – Series editors' introduction – Acknowledgements – List of abbreviations – **Part 1: An introduction to institutional self-study** Self-study and organizational learning Self-study in higher education – Self-study: A university perspective – **Part 2: Self-study in action** - The data cycle – The quality cycle – The planning cycle – **Part 3: The uses of self-study** – Self-study and decision-making – Self-study and reputation – An institutional balance sheet – References – Appendix 1: University of Brighton reports and documents – Appendix 2: Websites referred to in the text – Index.

2005 216pp

978 0 335 21502 7 Paperback